SOAR

SOAR

MY JOURNEY FROM COUNCIL ESTATE TO THE HOUSE OF LORDS

SIMON WOOLLEY

MANILLA
PRESS

First published in the UK by Manilla Press
an imprint of Bonnier Books UK
4th Floor, Victoria House
Bloomsbury Square,
London, WC1B 4DA
England

Owned by Bonnier Books
Sveavägen 56, Stockholm, Sweden

facebook.com/bonnierbooksuk/
twitter.com/bonnierbooks_uk

Hardback – 978-1-786-581-17-4
Ebook – 978-1-786-581-18-1
Audiobook – 978-1-786-581-19-8

A CIP catalogue of this book is available from the British Library.

Typeset by Envy Design Ltd

Printed and bound by Clays Ltd, Elcograf S.p.A

1 3 5 7 9 10 8 6 4 2

Copyright © Simon Woolley, 2022

First published in hardback by Manilla Press in 2022

Simon Woolley has asserted his moral right to be identified as the author of this
Work in accordance with the Copyright, Designs and Patents Act 1988.

Manilla Press is an imprint of Bonnier Books UK
www.bonnierbooks.co.uk

I dedicate this book, first to my two mothers: Lolita and Phyllis, aka Pippi. They are wonderful women who have had to fight throughout their lives but always remained loving. The latter is sadly no longer with us. Pippi essentially made me who I am today.

Lastly to my son, Luca. I can't love a human being more than this kid – who, by the way, is taller than me. He's humorous, smart, and full of bare-faced cheek, but loving with it.

I hope you're all as proud of me as much as I love you all.

CONTENTS

FOREWORD

BY THE REVEREND JESSE L. JACKSON, SR

It was a source of great pride to travel to Homerton College at Cambridge University to receive the prestigious Honorary Fellowship from my dear friend Lord Simon Woolley.

Bestowed a Fellowship from one of the great universities of the world is in and of itself a big deal, but for me this was much more than that. It was personal.

It was a landmark of an incredible journey initiated and witnessed by my friend, mentee and apprentice – call it what you will – come of age as a leader, something I knew he was always meant to be.

Our journey appropriately began more than twenty years prior in Atlanta, Georgia, fittingly home of my mentor Dr Martin Luther King, Jr., at the first State of the Black World conference organised by the great Ron Daniels.

Simon Woolley was the UK representative. He gave an accomplished speech that day, and wasn't fazed by the 2,000-strong audience or the stellar lineup of speakers, including Congresswoman Maxine Walters, Martin Luther King III, Danny Glover, and the Reverend Al Sharpton. But it was our conversations during those few days that convinced me that this was a young man who I wanted to mentor and above all collaborate with. He was that impressive!

He held a strong view, like me and many others, that racial injustice cannot be effectively tackled without political and indeed financial empowerment of Black communities around the world. Brother Woolley informed me that he wanted to emulate in the UK Dr King and his campaign of registering millions of African Americans to vote. His enthusiasm and energy was contagious. So, I agreed to travel to London and around the country to support Brother Woolley and his Operation Black Vote campaign on several occasions.

Every country and every civil rights campaigner has their own particular approach to confronting the lack of social, economic and political engagement of Black communities, and Woolley was no different, but he did share a lot of key tenets of my own organisation's makeup and mission in the Rainbow PUSH Coalition. Woolley's team spoke to the multicultural face of the UK with Africans, Asians, and Caribbeans all being a part of the OBV family. I got to know and love working with all of them. The irrepressible Lee Jasper, co-founder of OBV, Rita Patel, Karen Chouhan,

Audrey Adams, whose son Marlon was murdered by racist thugs back in 1980, Francine Fernandez, Winsome Cornish, and Ashok Viswanathan. It was a Rainbow team driven by the sole purpose of delivering racial justice.

My role was simple. Attract media attention, help bring together the various Black communities, and with Brother Woolley, explain that the vast majority of elections were won and lost by very small vote margins. In many close political races it was as clear as night-to-day that the Black vote could be the deciding factor.

Every general election I watched with immense pride as I witnessed the House of Commons become transformed with many more Black and Asian MPs. I knew very well the UK's first Black MPs Bernie Grant, Keith Vaz, Diane Abbott, and Paul Boateng, even before I got to know Brother Woolley, as the latter three have been my lifelong friends. But now the four MPs were becoming nine and then twenty-five, and now to what they are today, an unprecedented sixty-five. Lord Woolley and his team deserve a lot of the credit for massively moving these numbers.

I also recall with fondness how he would bring his political protégées from the UK and across Europe to the US for the annual Congressional Black Caucus Conference in Washington D.C., including one of Sweden's first male Black politicians, Momodou Jallow, Helen Grant MP, former equalities minister and first Conservative MP of African descent to be elected, Mayor Marvin Rees, first directly elected Mayor in Europe of Caribbean descent, former Shadow Minister Clive Lewis, and David Lammy, Shadow Justice Minster.

He told me the organisation's mission was twofold: 1: The British and other European MPs needed to see how Black America did big politics when more than 10,000 Black politicians gathered over four days to talk politics, business and give thanks to God; and 2: Equally important he wanted to showcase European talent to Black America.

Lord Woolley told the story of Mayor Marvin Rees, a descendent of an enslaved African who was now running the city of Bristol that had been at the epicentre of the barbaric human trade, and the audience rose as one to applaud the symbolism: from enslaved to governor for all, Black and white.

I would return again and again to the UK. In 2001, we combined a political and economic tour of the UK with a campaign bus tour fit for a king. In every city a huge crowd gathered to greet us, sometimes we'd visit two cities in a day. It was like being back on the 1984 and 1988 presidential campaign trail all over again. I loved it, and I loved being with them.

When you're a campaigner like Lord Woolley, like Karen Chouhan, you know budgets are low, and a lot of things get done on 'a wing and a prayer'. But they always got things done, and when things got tough I never once heard them argue as I've seen elsewhere with some activists.

I didn't know Brother Woolley's entire story until I read his book, and when you read it you'll have a greater appreciation of him as well. But what I did know is this, having watched and mentored this man over two decades, my mentor Dr King would not have hesitated in demanding that Brother Woolley join him as a key campaigner.

That's why I asked him to join me as one of my very special guests at the Élysée Palace when President Emanuel Macron awarded me their nation's highest honour: the Légion d'Honneur.

Lord Simon Woolley is not finished yet, not by a long way. His role as the first Black man to head an Oxbridge college is a new and exciting chapter to encourage and inspire generations to believe, no matter your race or your impoverished start in life you can and must succeed – dream beyond your circumstances. And in that success the goal is to bring others up to the decision-making tables to insist that political policies tackle poverty, inequality, and the scourge of global racism.

It has been my honour to know and work with Brother Woolley over many years. I look forward to doing so for many more years, keeping hope alive for others to follow. Brother Woolley continue to run a good race to serve and save humanity and will continue to soar.

Keep Hope Alive, Brother Woolley, Keep Hope Alive!

Rev. Jesse L. Jackson, Sr.
March, 2022

PROLOGUE

My name is Simon Woolley: Lord Woolley of Woodford, Kt, if you care to use my full title, which mostly I don't. I'm a crossbench peer, and principal of Homerton College, Cambridge; one of the first people of colour to lead an Oxbridge college. I'm the founder of Operation Black Vote, an organisation credited with encouraging tens of thousands of Black women and men to exercise their democratic right in the United Kingdom. I'm first generation British, of Barbadian Heritage. I grew up on an estate in Leicester, fostered by white parents at around two years old. I'm father to a son who makes me so proud I cry when I talk about him. My life has been hard, complicated, rich, varied, exciting and filled with adventures. It hasn't been easy, but today I can look back on what I've done with a sense of pride.

In the pages that follow, I'll take you on a journey back over my life, where I began and who I've become. Why? Because I hope that it might show young men and women in this country, whatever their background or heritage, that they too can shoot for the stars, take a chance, become the person they dream of being. When I was writing this book, I found myself looking back with a mixture of disbelief, wonder, pride and amazement at the man I've become and the place where I began.

Let's start with an image of me as a little boy, plain Simon Woolley, growing up on the St Matthew's estate in Leicester. There were very few Black families on the estate, and as I've said, my foster parents were white. At my school, I was one of only a handful of Black kids. I've been trying to think about when I first realised that I was Black; that race was an essential part of who I was. And when I cast my mind back, I remember Ian Harding, another Black kid from St Matthew's, and me, running together.

Our Cubs group was invited to a Jamboree when I was about nine. It was an all-day event, and we took part in a variety of games, including the three-legged race. I was twinned with Ian Harding, who I knew because he was looked after by my mum in exchange for dodgy bespoke clothes. My mum took in other kids from the estate and often took payment in kind if the parents had no cash to pay her in a particular week. Ian's mum sewed truly awful clothes, which my brother and I often ended up wearing because there was so little money spare. I was pleased to be paired with Ian, because he was fast, *very* fast. He played football for England as a schoolboy, until his dad put the blockers on because he didn't do his homework and was falling behind. And I was no slouch either; I knew I was fast. We stood there, arms around each other, legs tied together. I glanced from side to side: there were four pairs of boys on our left, three on our right. All white kids. Then Ian and me in the middle. We looked at each other and nodded. The scout leader gave the signal and we were off. We started tentatively slow, just finding our rhythm, but as we moved through gears our stride lengthened, our pace became fierce: suddenly we were moving together, flying as one, sprinting as individuals, but bound together, with a common purpose and a determination to win. No one was ahead of us, and we couldn't hear anyone close behind. We seemed to run alone down the track. As we crossed the finish line, we glanced back. A number of the boys had fallen over and were lying in tangled heaps along the track: the few still running were so far behind, it was embarrassing. We looked at each other and grinned. Ian and I got a lot of shit for being boys of colour in a very white neighbourhood, but we were used to putting up with it. We each knew already, at a very young age, just to get on with it and be the best we could be. But that day I suddenly I had this glorious sense, at a time when I really needed it, of pride. As we'd flown along, brothers together, heads down, running fast, I'd understood that there was something very special about being Black, supporting each other.

Together, we can soar.

CHAPTER 1

IT BEGINS LIKE THIS

An old photo. A fleeting conversation. A memory.

One of the many things that have always fascinated me about human beings is our recollection of childhood. But, of course, you're never really sure how much you genuinely remember about growing up, are you? Even in an age of non-stop social media, where anyone under twenty-five is the star of their very own version of *The Truman Show*, what you think you remember from all those photos, films, videos and family stories about your childhood is one thing. But what do you really remember? What is the first thing that you held on to, that imprinted itself indelibly in your mind, even if only as a brief moment, a single image? A real memory, not filtered through a sepia-tinged photograph, dog-eared newspaper or washed-out Polaroid? Did I really go there? Did she really say that? Is that how it was?

My very first memory, I can say with as much certainty as it is possible to have about this sort of thing, is of being in the back of a car – I was probably two, going on three years of age, maybe.

Even though I've loved cars for as long as I can remember, the make or model of this particular vehicle eludes my memory, as does the person who was driving. I distinctly remember looking out of the rear window at a group of people standing on the pavement, gradually fading from view. I was going from one place to another. From one family to another. From one life to another.

* * *

My mother Lolita arrived in Britain in 1957 from Barbados, a small island and, then, a tiny corner of the 'Empire', in an area known as the West Indies. She was seventeen years old and she had come to work as a nurse in the rapidly expanding National Health Service. Lolita was part of what we now call the 'Windrush generation' – those who emigrated to Britain from the Caribbean between 1948 and 1971, encouraged by the British government to fill post-war labour shortages. She remembers that it was Enoch Powell, infamous for his 'Rivers of Blood' speech, who was the government minister who came to my mother's small island pleading for young, smart, strong talent to come and do their bit. She had never set foot in Britain before but she didn't see her new home as a foreign country. Lolita was a full British citizen; as she disembarked from the ship, she held in her hand a British passport. She and her fellow passengers were travelling from the islands where they were born to the 'mother country' – the heart of the empire of which they were a part. And they were following in the footsteps of the tens of thousands of Caribbean men who had volunteered to fight for Britain in the Second World War, fewer than two decades before. Whether standing up to the Nazis or working in the NHS, that generation saw their role or 'duty' within the British Empire.

Each Barbadian citizen had to have a British sponsor, and my mum's lived in Melton Mowbray in Leicestershire. The young seventeen-year-old stayed with a family who owned a small restaurant, where my mother worked for a while. The family were desperate for her to stay on, she was after all a 'good grafter', but young Lolita would not be deterred from her life's mission in England: to become a nurse. So one day she turned to the head of the house and said, 'I've come to the UK to be a nurse, and that's what I'm going to do.' And with that, she signed up to become one of the tens of thousands of Caribbean nurses that have worked in the NHS, first at Hillcrest old people's home, then for most of her adult life at the Royal Infirmary in the city centre.

Lolita settled in Leicester and met my older brother's father, who was a white man. They married and had their first son but within a few years, the marriage broke down and they separated. This was a time when both 'alternative parenting' and interracial relationships or multicultural families were hugely frowned upon. She would later tell me that the local Barbadian community's message to her after her separation was, 'Look, we told you to keep to your own and this is what you should have done.'

So, now alone with a child and still only in her early twenties, she duly had a fling with one of 'her own'. Lolita became pregnant, with me, but my father wasn't told. He never knew, and my mother doesn't want to talk about it. There is a story, I'm not sure how true it is, that my father returned to the Caribbean, had his own family and lived out a good life, oblivious to the knowledge of his real firstborn, back in England.

So Lolita was a single mother in the 1960s, struggling with two kids, a long way from where she had grown up.

Then, Lolita's ex, my older brother's father, wanted to return to the family home and rekindle their relationship. I'm not sure if by this time Lolita was pregnant with my younger brother, but her husband would only come back on one condition: I had to go.

Lolita had to choose between being a single mother with three kids or life with her husband and two of her children.

And so I was taken in by an orphanage run by Catholic nuns.

* * *

Going somewhere in a car would have been a fairly unusual event for a poor kid in Leicester in the early 1960s. Perhaps that's why it stayed stuck in my memory when so many other details from my childhood have gone. Or perhaps I knew that I was going somewhere important. That life was about to start again.

As was the usual practice, the nuns had put me up for adoption via the local council. And an older, white couple, Phyllis and Daniel Fox, had responded. They were to be my foster parents and it was to their house I was being taken in the back of the car.

Phyllis and Daniel lived on the St Matthew's council estate, now one of the poorest in England. Work had started on the housing development in 1958, replacing the back-to-back, two-up, two-down terraces that Victorian landlords had thrown up to house the city's industrial workforce. The intentions may have been good – at its inception, the local paper referred to it as 'the silver lining estate' – but the execution, as with so many council estates all around Britain, was not. For one, it was isolated, with no adjacent residential areas, and cut off from the city centre by the dual carriageway ring road. But back then these were working-class estates where people looked after their homes and gardens, places where the overwhelming majority of people worked, and worked hard.

For us, the estate was our playground, not just the 'little or big park' where you could play football or swings, but more interesting, the high walls to climb on, the flat roof sheds, not only to scale but to show your daring by jumping across from one to another. The Pyatt brothers were good at this, as was Wayne McNeil, although the latter did come unstuck trying a particular jump. 'You're never going to make it,' we jeered up at him, and guess what, he didn't, and bust his leg. But we were proud of him for having a go.

All the houses on the estate were virtually the same: downstairs kitchen and lounge, upstairs two bedrooms and a bathroom, oh, and a coal shed just outside the front for the coalman to deliver our winter fuel. Just think about that for second. What a back-breaking job! Delivering bags of coal to hundreds of houses a day. I mean, I used to hate it when my mum – my new mum – would shout, 'Simon, go and fetch me a bucket of coal!' Me and my adoptive brother, Mick, had to do many jobs around the house, this was not one of the favourites. None of them were, but you know what I mean. The coal was wedged in a shute in a cupboard outside and with a piece of wood tilted up to allow all the round coke pieces to come out of the bottom. My job was to get a small shovel and pick up what I could and allow more to fall to the bottom to start again. Once the bucket was full you shut the outside cupboard, making sure you hadn't left an unholy mess, or woe betide you, and then with great balancing skill, you would take it inside and Mum would do the rest. She removed the safety grill, put some paper on the base, then the coal and somehow, like magic, a warm glowing fire would appear.

All the houses were more or less the same, no one in our neighbourhood was any poorer or richer than anyone else. Of course, there was the odd exception when Tom and John Graig's mum got them a colour TV – now that was a big deal – or when, my best friend for ages, Richard Fizakely, was bought a Raleigh Chopper for Christmas. It was like seeing an object from outer space, it was that cool.

My father, Daniel – Dan, who, sadly, I never called Father, which is a monster regret of mine – was a hulking Irishman, a big set man with huge hands. He would ritually sit in 'his' chair, which would bulge and expand around his huge frame like a Muscle Fit T-shirt. Old-fashioned braces held up his trousers, and his big black slip-on shoes were always clean. He was a man of few needs: he liked his dinner ready when he got home; you wouldn't dare be sat in his chair when he arrived back from work, and at the weekend, he'd like his half-bottle of whisky, which back then me and my brother could buy for him from the 'Indian shop' across the road. He was something of a gentle giant who never lifted a finger to me or my adoptive brother, Mick. But he'd give us 'the look' and, such was his quiet authority, that was all that was needed.

While Daniel was, in keeping with men of that generation, somewhat removed or detached from my everyday life, Phyllis – Pippi – was ever-present. She was very good with people, very sociable, and even better with kids. In fact, she looked after loads of kids, including me and Mick.

Being taken in by the Foxes meant being in a house filled with children and love. Mick – Michael Wright – and I knew we weren't blood brothers, but I did consider him to be my older brother. He was three years older than me, and of mixed heritage – 'half-caste' they used to say in those less enlightened times. Mick had been at Phyllis and Daniel's place for a year or so before I arrived and my appearance was not wholly welcomed by a little boy who was only just starting to feel sure of himself in his new home.

The couple had fostered children before either of us had appeared on the scene. As I said, Pippi loved children. Whether she was child-minding or fostering, she gave, I guess, hundreds of kids the love they could not get from their biological parents. If you were a registered foster parent and child-minder you received money from the government for taking in children; it wasn't a lot but if you loved kids, you could pocket a little extra cash to make sure you made ends meet, which was always a challenge.

Our house was always full of kids during the school term. A host of mothers would leave their children at our place in the morning; Mick and I would take them to school, marshalling our little troop through the estate, then, at the end of the day, I'd wait for them and take them back to our place, where sandwiches and homemade cakes would be laid on for tea. They'd spend a couple of hours wreaking havoc until the mums came and collected them after work or I'd drag them all over to the local park. 'Go on, take 'em out for an hour,' Pippi would say. Mick and I were part of the team – you pulled your weight. I remember being six or seven and taking the younger kids to nursery or primary school on my own. I remember my school teacher Mrs Webb being more than a little impressed with my young leadership skills: 'You, young man, are going to be someone very special, very important with those skills. But you make sure you're not late for class!'

* * *

When Pippi first met Dan, she had worked in service, like many of their generation. She was originally from the mining valleys of Wales and when the daughters of the Valleys were old enough, as was the custom, they would be sent away to work in service as maids or nannies. The Foxes had two grown-up daughters, Maureen and Patricia, both of whom had long since married and moved away. As they were much older than me, I came to see them as aunties rather than big sisters. When Maureen and Patricia were young, Pippi wanted to send them back to the Valleys to stay with her grandmother while she worked in service, so the two daughters left for South Wales. However, her eldest, Pat, had pined for her mother so much that she came back to Leicester. She couldn't bear to be without her and so the two daughters had very different lives. Pat was practically shackled to my mum, to an almost detrimental extent, because she was unable to be fully independent. A marriage breakup and lack of self-belief drained the lifeblood of this once vivacious young woman. In contrast, Maureen, who stayed in Wales to be brought up by my grandma and my auntie Bess, excelled in living; met an American GI, emigrated to the US and lived a full and very different life.

My dad was a quiet man except when he was swearing about politics and power dynamics. 'The weak and wicked,' he would curse. I never knew his politics but I'm sure it was Labour. I remember Greville Janner, who we'd see during election time driving around in a car with a loudspeaker on top, blaring out the same message – 'Vote Labour, Vote Greville Janner!'

When it came to matters of the heart, my dad had only one simple unequivocal piece of advice for me and my brother, which only surfaced after he and Pippi had been arguing over something trivial. 'Boys,' he'd say, with a knowing resignation, 'never get married,' before adding with a irresistible wry smile, 'Oh, and two sugars in my tea, please.'

Dan, was a foreman at Dunlop Tyres in Leicester. He was never ill – not that I can recall – and never missed a day's work, with the one exception, when he'd drunk a little too much Johnnie Walker, slipped on the stairs and broke his arm. When he would come home from work, me and my brother would be waiting for him to emerge from the street corner. He'd dig deep into his pocket and out from there would come two 'Bar Sixes'. They were like Kit-Kats and they had six sections of chocolate.

But it was my mum who was the life and soul of our household. We had an old reel-to-reel tape recorder with big spools and a microphone. We'd wheel it out for special occasions – it was our version of karaoke. My mum would sing 'Danny Boy' with passion, but a not altogether perfect pitch. She'd also sing at the annual Old People's Concert organised by Mrs Franklin. She even roped in me and

Mick to sing songs such as 'Oh, You Beautiful Doll' and '(How Much Is) That Doggie In The Window.' I once asked Mrs Franklin if I could sing a rendition of Michael Jackson's 'Ben'. To be fair, she let me sing it to her and then diplomatically said no. Whether it was me not quite hitting the high notes, or maybe it was just too modern for the pensioners, I'll never know.

What I do know is that my mum was a true community champion, whether it was helping out with the church jumble sale and getting first dibs on clothes for Mick and me, or entertaining the old folks. That's what she did. She *was* the local community. She was child-minder, singer, entertainer and Mother Teresa rolled into one.

When I look at the oldest-surviving pictures of me from that era, there are two that really stand out. In the first one, the very earliest photo of me, I had just arrived in the house. Daniel has his arms around me, this little Black child with what can only be described as an expression of unknowing and lack of belonging. Daniel's wearing a big shirt, trademark dark trousers and braces. With his huge arms around me it's the very image of a protective gesture, yet my face is as sullen and lonely as it can be.

The second picture is of me some time later. I'd just started at the local primary school and I'd settled into the organised chaos of home life. Now, you see a totally different child, the face of a child that would feature in every single picture from that point onwards. I have a smart dicky bow and an ear-to-ear beaming smile, I look like the cat that got the cream. Something changed dramatically. I was quickly made to feel that I belonged. I now had a sense of being part of a family, a real family. I was no longer the Black sheep, the outcast: I was simply Simon.

And yet, I never called Phyllis 'Mum', even though she treated me like a son and I think of her as my mother. The smallest of the kids she looked after called her 'Pippi' as they couldn't pronounce Phyllis, and so did I. We had different last names: hers was Fox and mine was Woolley and it was clear to anyone looking at us that we were not related. But the bond between Pippi and me was irrefutable; she was undoubtedly the single biggest influence on me.

She was also my protector, and a fierce one at that. There was one time, when I was five or six, I was playing in the 'little park' and a group of boys stole my football. I ran home crying to Pippi. She took me by the arm and we strode back down to the park. Rather than go through the main gate, Pippi took the shortcut we kids would use, through a tiny gap in the park's mesh fence.

'I'm gonna deal with this!' she snarled, 'I'm gonna deal with it!'

To this day, I don't know how she got through that fence because it seemed almost physically impossible, given her size. But I clearly remember the determination on her face: *how do I get to these bullies who are giving my kid a hard time and have nicked his ball in the quickest possible fashion?* So she got through the hole in the fence, clambered through the bushes, saw the group of boys and screamed, 'Oi, you! Give my boy his ball back . . . NOW!' The tone of her voice was so piercing and so frightening that the kids just dropped the ball and ran off. The next thing I knew, I was walking back home with her, she had her arm around me, I had my ball and all was right in the world.

* * *

You don't need to be very old to start to understand where you are in the socio-economic pecking order. Kids pick this up (and internalise it) from an early age. As I said before, generally we all had pretty much the same, which might not have been a great deal but when everyone else in is a similar position you don't know any different. But I was aware that at times it was challenging for us. It was never spoken about, and me and my brother were massively shielded from most of it, but even a child can pick up on things. On more than one occasion, I saw my mother steal food when we went shopping. She would put a shawl over the eggs or some other food in the trolley and deliberately not pay for it. She never knew that I'd spotted her doing it or, if she did, she never let on. There was no way that she would have wanted to make me complicit. Yet, for all that, my brother and I had bikes; we had Christmas presents. We were poor but not in the depths of poverty. We never went hungry and never had a miserable Christmas. But it was clear that my mother made sacrifices and counted the pennies to make sure that my brother and I had all the basics. But, I realised, this isn't what it means to be poor. This is what it means to make ends meet, and that means counting the pennies – and occasionally watching your mum steal food from Tesco's. Thankfully, today, foodbanks help ensure that mums like mine don't have to steal to properly feed their families.

Mick and I were nearly always dressed the same in those early years, either in handmade clothes or hand-me-downs, but we were always dressed identically, like twins. A few mothers whose children my mum looked after couldn't always afford to pay her fees, so they would make clothes for Mick and me as payment in kind.

For example, Ian and Dawn Harding's mum was a seamstress and she'd make us the most dreadful outfits. They were made of corduroy or velvet or whatever polyester odds and ends the women had lying around. We had these awful trousers, which were just like sailors' trousers, all baggy and ill-fitting, along with matching waistcoats. But we never quibbled about wearing them. You might think that I'm wearing fancy dress in the photo on the cover of this book – it's not, it's one of Mrs Harding's creations.

Taylor Street Primary and Junior School was an overwhelmingly white school. I was the only Black child in my year and one of the very few children of colour at all. There was my older brother, Mick, and maybe one or two others. Overall, my memories of school were very positive. I was fairly bright – I mean, not top of the class, but up there. I had my friends, Richard Fizakely, John Jones and Michael Webbe, and like all the boys in the class, we were all in love with Maria Holland, who lived on the 'New' estate that emerged in the late 1960s on St Matthew's.

I had my run-ins with a few boys. One in particular was a kid who had a reputation for being the best fighter in the school, Wayne Foster. He would bully me relentlessly. One day, when I was about seven or eight, I went home and told my brother. Mick seldom taught me anything, he was too busy with his own life, but he did teach me how to fight.

Mick was bigger and stronger than me, plus he had a shocking temper, truly frightening. Sometimes I would try and fight back, but I could never match his inner rage, and I just couldn't beat him. Fighting Mick taught me that physically, at least, there's always somebody that can beat you no matter what you do, no matter how strong you are or how resilient you can be. Part of Mick's anger and, dare I say, disquiet towards me, stemmed from the fact that not only was he also fostered and was thus wrestling with his own sense of rejection, but to make matters worse, here I was, the new kid on the block, three years younger, the interloper again, taking away some of the attention my brother richly deserved.

Just before she died in 1982, I asked my mum why Mick had given me a hard time. 'I don't fully know,' she said. 'He was a good kid and now he's a very good father, but the truth was, you were easy to love, Simon.' I thought, *wow*. If my brother internalised any of that, no wonder I was never going to be his favourite. I deeply love my brother now and for a long time, but those early years and difficulties meant that back then, we were not close.

But he must have felt some sort of responsibility towards me because he taught me exactly what to do to stop this bully from pushing me around. Mick said, 'When Wayne Foster hits you or goes to hit you, pull back and then you punch him as hard as you possibly can.' So, the next day, I was in the playground when Wayne came over to me and started on me again. At first, I took it: the pushing, the shoving, the abuse. But then when he went to hit me, I moved to the side, slipping his punch, and then hit him a couple of times, hard, really hard. Within seconds, I'd beaten the hardest kid in the school. It was like that moment in old myths or fairy tales when he who beats the King becomes the King. It was a life-changing moment – at least, at that age. The all-important hierarchy of the playground was rearranged. It felt like Muhammad Ali, looking down on a floored Sonny Liston.

Wayne staggered to his feet, just about holding back the tears, but enough for him to run away through a crowd of kids, who only a few seconds before were chanting, 'Fight, fight, fight!' There was the jockeying, the pats on the back, the recognition. I'd gone from being the one who was bullied in school to now being respected. I was now seen as the best fighter of my year and then, as I got to the last year of primary school, I was regarded as the de facto best fighter in the school. In truth, I was no Muhammad Ali. At primary school, I probably had about three fights in total and they lasted a matter of seconds but it didn't matter. As far as anyone was concerned, I was not to be messed with. 'Simon Woolley is a big fat bully,' some of the girls would chant. Nevertheless, I was always afraid that if there was somebody tough – I mean, really tough, just like my brother, Mick – I'd get found out. But I never did.

Growing up a Black fostered kid in a largely white community, I experienced plenty of occasions when it was made abundantly clear to me that my skin colour was a problem for some. But then there were other times when I perhaps didn't notice or didn't understand what was going on. For example, the experience of being 'othered' was much more subtle, more insidious. I remember being at our local church as a choir boy during a wedding. Someone from the wedding party called me over and asked if I would have a picture with the lucky couple. There I am in my homemade clothes and there's this group of white people all dolled up to the nines, beckoning me over for a photo op. I thought, *What? Why would they want a picture with me? Why?* Well, apparently, it was good luck for the newly married couple. There was a tradition, which apparently dates back to the eighteenth century, when a chimney sweep saved King George III – the passing monarch's horse bolted and the gallant sweep managed to bring it to a halt. The King then sent for a chimney sweep to attend his daughter's wedding, for good luck, and the idea stuck. It's customary for the chimney sweep to shake the groom's hand and kiss the bride, as a lucky omen. I got collared a number of times to be a chimney sweep at a wedding. At that age, I was just happy to be the centre of attention, but looking back it seems, well, it is a bit shocking, demeaning. But by the same token, it was endearing because it was naïve and innocent, and no harm or offence was intended. There were far more worrying forms of racism that we would have to worry about than being likened to a chimney sweep.

And I do like the idea that someone, somewhere probably still has a wedding photo with a future Lord of the Realm, masquerading as a chimney sweep outside St Matthew's Church, Leicester.

* * *

Looking back at many of these childhood events, I'm kind of convinced I had a number of traits that I've mostly carried through to this very day: Being hungry to achieve; I'd always go the extra mile; I loved the hustle; wheeling and dealing, ducking and diving; and I wanted to win, not at any price, but I did always want to win.

While at primary school, I joined the Cub Scouts. I had to wear a cap and baggy shorts and carry out various tasks to get badges. One of my favourite Cubs' activities was 'bob-a-job week', which involved going around the estates, knocking on people's doors and talking them into paying you a 'bob', or five pence, to do a simple job, like taking out their rubbish, washing their car or chopping up wood. You'd knock on a door, smile and say, 'It's bob-a-job week, do you have any jobs?' and then people would give you a job, you would collect the money, go back to the Cubs with all your change and hand it over to the Scout Leader. I have no idea what they did with the money – pay the rent on the premises, I guess. Anyway, that wasn't my issue. My goal was to come back with the most money at the end of the week. I couldn't have been much older than eight or nine then. So off I'd go, knocking on people's doors at the weekend from sun-up to sundown, often going far afield, too. For me, distance didn't matter and, shockingly now when you think about it, neither did being alone, but there it was, it was a different time. Not that horrible things didn't happen to kids my age, it's just that we weren't wrapped up in cotton wool, like I have done for my one and only son. Back then in our little groups/gangs we instinctively knew who the man was to avoid. You know, the one that sat in the 'little park' with his mac on, watching the kids. We'd throw stones at him and chase him out of the park.

Back to bob-a-job… I'd been working my socks off on our estate and strayed on to another off the Belgrave Road in Leicester, a shabby part of the city with lots of two-up, two-down rough terraced houses that still had the toilet in the backyard. Very few homes had toilets inside the house, they were that old and dilapidated. The door opened and I said, beaming, 'Bob-a-job week.' The man said, 'Yeah, OK, come in the back.'

The back of this house was filthy. It made Steptoe and Son's home look regal. Looking back at it now, it was a safeguarding nightmare, yet the potential dangers of sending kids off to dodgy spaces with even dodgier individuals was clearly not properly thought through. Finally, this guy said to me, 'OK, I'll give you a few pence if you clear my backyard.' Christ! This backyard was so full of rubbish — piles of boxes, books, cans and bottles and all manner of detritus filled the place. I thought, *You've got to be kidding*. But nevertheless, I did it — I spent quite a few hours clearing this shitty backyard, sweating buckets. I walked out of there looking like I'd slept on a landfill site all week, with the smell to boot, and whether I got five bob or ten bob, I can't remember now — I know that I got a lot, and I bloody earned it!

But by the end of bob-a-job week, when I sat on my bed at home and emptied out the rusty old tin containing all the cash I'd earned — the copper coins, the silver coins, counting it into pound piles — I knew I'd done well. I walked to Cubs with a big grin on my face and poured all the money I'd earned onto a table in front of the Scout Leader. I must've raised about £10, which was a lot of money back then, an awful lot of money just for doing odd jobs. Bear in mind that in 1970, the average weekly wage for a full-time, male manual worker aged twenty-one and over was around £28, and just under £14 for women aged eighteen and over.

The money was one thing, but it was the sense of achievement that really mattered. I'd won, and I guess I wanted approval from adults. Maybe I wanted to be loved, I don't know. Let's not get too deep: I was just being me.

CHAPTER 2

BOY FROM
ST MATTHEW'S

This is a bit difficult to write, but I'll give it a go.

Pippi did tell me about my birth mother and I was aware that I had an older brother. Sometimes I'd look at older Black boys, particularly the big strong and handsome ones, and ponder: 'Maybe that's my brother. Maybe I'll look like that when I grow up. I hope so.'

Around this time, my birth mother, Lolita, somehow got word to Pippi and Dan and asked them if I'd like to go back and live with her. I brushed off the request and said, 'No, of course not. I don't want to go.' I mean, think about it. Go back to who? I had no memory of my mother or brother for that matter, so what was I going back to?

Then, when I was in my teens, after ten or twelve years of living with them, my foster parents had the opportunity to legally adopt me.

'Would you like that?' asked Pippi.

'I'd like nothing more,' I said.

'Right, OK.'

And that was that. The funny thing is, even after the formal adoption went through, I didn't change my name and nor did my brother, who, like me, was also fostered then adopted by the Foxes. I feel a little guilty about that now, as after all these years, I always refer to Pippi as my mother.

* * *

I started at Ellis Boys' Comprehensive School in September 1972. On my very first day, I got into a fight with a boy in the second year, Micky Hughes. So there I was, a lowly first year, probably wearing platform shoes, Farah trousers and a Ben Sherman shirt, standing in the canteen queue at dinner time, and somebody pushed me. I turned around and it was just this stupid-looking kid. *For Christ's sake*, I thought, *this is my first day at school and I can't catch a break.*

'Get out of the way,' the kid snarled.

'*You* get out of the way,' I snapped back. 'I was here first.'

He then tried to hit me but missed, so I hit him. And that was it: the fight was over.

Soon, the word got about – 'This first-year kid is a tough nut.' So that fight on the first day of school made other kids wary of having a go at me. Soon, my reputation was preceding me and instantly I was again 'the best fighter' in my year, which was nonsense really, but it put me in good stead as these were the days in school when you really had to prove yourself; you had to hit the ground running, particularly so if you were a minority in that area. You could be good-looking, or maybe you were seen as a bit of a smooth operator, or perhaps you were good at sport – or you were a good fighter. I was perceived as a good fighter and good at sport, from football to running to rugby – that was my cachet. When I think back to my school days now, fighting was writ large: you just had to be able to fight.

I had a motley crew of friends from the St Matthew's estate. There was Raymond Pyatt and his brother Chris (who would later become WBO world middleweight boxing champion), and Greg Bannon, Tucker Watts, Mark Felts, Wayne McNeil and Savvas Demetriou, who is still one of my best friends to this day. Like many Greek Cypriots at that time, his family had a fish and chip shop. We didn't call him Savvas, though, we called him 'Simon' and that's all I ever knew him as. So few of us at school were from non-white or non-British backgrounds and, like most kids, all we wanted to do was 'belong'. So for twenty-five years or more, I knew Savvas as 'Simon'. Then one day he said to me, 'Simon, don't call me Simon any more. I'm Savvas, OK?' He owned his proud Greek-Cypriot ethnicity, which I thought was great.

We got up to all sorts. Life was a series of scrapes and capers, adventures and near-misses that set us apart from everyone else. All of us were into hustling. We were always trying to find a way to earn some money and make our own entertainment. We'd 'find' old beer bottles or those

Corona fizzy drinks bottles and take them back to the off-licence or the delivery truck and get the deposits on them. You had to hustle, you had to learn how to navigate trouble or to see an opportunity. You learned how to think on your feet. I did things at twelve years old that my fifteen-year-old son couldn't even dream about doing because children are so cosseted these days. I think about when we were nine years old and we'd go to the park and know who the nonce was, instantly. As I've said, we'd throw stones at him. When you think about it, it's insane. We were nine years old and throwing stones at a paedophile in the park. But we were always in a group, in a gang. We had safety in numbers.

By the time we were twelve we'd developed a 'nice little earner'. We'd all head down to Filbert Street, home of Leicester City Football Club, on a match day and buy and sell match tickets. So there we were, these twelve-year-old urchins at a football ground with hooligans, who were often racists, buying and selling match tickets like a right bunch of wide boys.

It took me a year to find out who had the tickets but eventually I wound up with two serious sources. One was the youth team players who were thirteen, fourteen and fifteen. As junior members of the Leicester City set-up, they would get complimentary match tickets to give to their family and friends. I'd butter up these lads and buy their tickets for about 50 pence to £1 for each one. Each player was allocated five tickets by the club, so it'd cost me a maximum of £5 per player. I'd sell the tickets outside the ground on a match day for a maximum of a fiver each. I soon became a seasoned ticket tout. These youth players, including Paul Ramsey, who went on to play for Northern Ireland, and other players who went on to play senior football, would come out of the ground before the game with the tickets, and Ramsey would see me and quip, 'Aye, aye! Here comes the *big man*. The big man's coming.' I'd hand them a fiver each, take the tickets and say, 'See you next week.'

Another source was a guy called Moose, who was friends with all the big-time players – Frank Worthington, Alan Birchenall, Keith Weller, he knew them all. They would give him tickets; he would give them to me. Everyone got paid.

Once all the tickets were sold, we'd go and watch the game. Of course we wouldn't pay; under the turnstile we'd go. Or give the guy on the gate a few quid and we'd be in. We'd get a hot drink and a pie, sit in the corner and count our money while we ate our food. We'd generally watch a bit of the game and then leave at half-time. We rarely stayed to watch the whole thing. We would go into town, buy some clothes, go to someone's house and play cards – usually three-card brag, which, frankly, I was hopeless at and would lose most of my money, usually to the Pyatt brothers. But with a bit of luck, I would go home with 20 or 30 quid in my pocket from the day's work.

Most Saturday evenings after a match, once I got home, I'd go and find Mum. I'd give her a fiver and I'd say, 'This is for you, Pippi. It's for you to go and get your hair done.' She'd smile, fold it up and tuck it in her apron pocket. On one occasion, I gave her some money and she took a step back, surveyed me and said, 'Simon, I don't worry about you; you're going to be fine, you're going to be fine.' Patently, she knew something I didn't.

I spent much of my youth in and around Filbert Street, hanging around, touting outside that old football ground. But the other caper that took up much of my spare time was sneaking into the cinema. There must have been at least three cinemas in Leicester in those days and my ragtag gang of mates and I would rotate around them, particularly in the winter, primarily to get out of the cold. If it was a good film, we'd watch it, but the main attraction – apart from central heating – was using our wit and guile to sneak into the pictures. Another part of the game was watching good films and then spoiling it for people because we'd talk all the way through, telling the paying punters what was going to happen. A terrific film like *Jaws*, for instance. I must've watched it about forty times. I was a few months shy of my fourteenth birthday when it was released in the summer of 1975. It's hard to describe just how massive it was then; it was *everywhere*. It became the first movie to earn $100 million at the box office and is generally considered the first-ever blockbuster. There's a terrifying moment in the film when Richard Dreyfuss goes diving at night to check out a shipwreck and the head of a missing fisherman comes rolling out of a hole in the boat, and his eye pops out – aargh! My mates and I would spoil it for the whole audience – what were we thinking? We were right little shits! But that was all part of the fun.

Sneaking into the pictures was an art and the most gifted artist was Tucker Watts. Wayne McNeil wasn't bad – but Tucker was the King. To get into the local cinema you would get a coat hanger, put it in between the gap of the emergency exit door and then twist it around and lift the bar that was behind the door. The door would magically swing open and we'd all just look at each other, laughing. It took great skill, great finesse to open that door, and Tucker was the key. Sometimes, we'd even wind up in some dingy porno cinema with the dirty mac brigade. Occasionally, we'd clock a grown-up we knew in there: 'It's Mr Whitehead, the youth leader. Oi! Mr Whitehead!'

On one occasion, we snuck into the movies, hunkered down at the back of the cinema and my friend Michael Webb started nudging me in the ribs.

'Webby, shut up, watch the film, watch the film,' I whispered, shooing him away. 'Watch the film, you're gonna get us chucked out.'

'No, Simon, look, look!' Michael shot back, gesturing over his shoulder. I turned around and saw my form teacher, Miss Hill, sat there with her boyfriend. She looked at me. I looked straight up and thought, *oh gosh, now I'm in trouble, she's seen us all sneak in.*

The next day, I walked into class expecting an earful.

'Simon, can you come to the front, please,' Miss Hill said, giving me daggers.

I thought, *I'm so in trouble now.*

'You were in the cinema yesterday, weren't you?'

'Yes, miss, yes, miss. I'm really sorry, miss, I can explain . . .'

'No, no, no . . . I want you to give us all a synopsis of the film you saw.'

I can't now remember what film it was but I was very relieved not to be in trouble and I was able to wax lyrical about the plot and the acting. From that day on, I was the class film critic . . . for the next few weeks at least! Miss Hill would call me to the front and say, 'Simon, have you seen any good films lately? Can you give us a movie review?'

I was in my element, holding court. It was brilliant.

* * *

Being a Black kid in a white school with all-white teachers was like being a guinea pig in a social experiment. But even so, looking back now, I find it difficult to say how much racism there was at school, from the teachers. How their expectations of me may have been different to white pupils with the same level of ability as me. This is largely because very few of the kids were pushed to do great things at school. You just went to school, came home and did your homework as best you could. There was no oversight from your parents; they were busy working to pay the rent. Almost all our parents worked in factories or did manual labour and there was no reason for them to think that we'd be any different. The only time they had off was the July fortnight when the whole town would go to Mablethorpe Beach or Skegness. You were encouraged to get a manual job. Parents and teachers had no great expectations of us, and we had few aspirations above and beyond the microcosmic world we inhabited.

A few of the teachers didn't like me and some of them punished me because I was a prick. There was a guy called Mr Scranioch, who was a bit of a shocker. He was an ex-Leicester City rugby player who took particular delight in picking me up by the lapels, putting me against the wall and giving me a whack. You have to bear in mind that it was the mid-1970s and it was still open season on corporal punishment, but even by those standards this guy was harsh. But do I think there was any racial intent? I don't think so but I don't honestly recall. Which could of course have been my self-preservation mechanism.

The one exception was sport. As with any Black kid of that era, the teachers expected me to be good at sport. They thought 'Black' and they thought 'athletic'. And that was about it. And I was good at sport. To which the question naturally follows, would I have been better at other things too if I'd have felt the expectation was there that I was capable, that I had the potential? Would all of us?

I was captain of the football team, athletics team and the basketball team. What few Black kids there were at my school all figured heavily in sports, which gave us status at school but of course reinforced a flattering but also problematic stereotype of us being 'naturally athletic', while ignoring what we might achieve academically.

When I was eleven or twelve, I had a trial for Leicester City. At that age, boy was I fast! In primary school, I wanted to be an attacker, despite having started off being in defence. At the back, I could just command the defence because nobody could outpace me, so when I went for the trial for Leicester City, I started off as a fullback, playing out wide. I was completely in control. It was just easy. I could read the game well and knew how to attack and show a little bit of skill with the ball. So, I had this trial for about half an hour and I just felt like *this is a breeze.* Then suddenly, pow, bang, shit! I pulled my hamstring – I'd never even realised what it was before.

'You can't carry on playing, son,' the coach said as I hobbled off the pitch. I skulked off to the dressing room, got my kit on, got the bus and went back home. No doctors, no one came to look at me; I just hobbled home. Back at school, the sports teacher said to me, 'Leicester said you were very, very good, and they want to get back in touch with you because they feel that you can be part of the set-up.' But back then, you never went home and told your parents anything. You just went for a game and that was it. Anyway, nobody pushed it. Neither the school, nor my parents. So it just fizzled away and I never got a second chance. I've always felt that if I'd had a good coach in those days they would have said, 'Yes, we want you to go for it,' and they would have followed it up.

So, the football opportunity and the dream of being the next Pele, albeit in defence, came and went. I carried on playing football for local teams, but without being on professional scouts' radar in that space, you were never going to progress. That was just the way it was. If you managed to get into the system, you had a chance of a life-changing shot at professional football; if not, you had to make do playing schoolboy Sunday league football with your mates. If you were lucky, you'd go on to be builders, plasterers and plumbers, then wind up playing adult Sunday league, moaning about what could have been. To quote Marlon Brando's character in the Hollywood classic, *On the Waterfront*, 'I coulda been a contender . . .'

We all used to go boxing, primarily because of former European champion Tony Sibson, who trained at a boxing club in Melton Road. Me, the Pyatt brothers, Tucker Watts and Savvas. We loved it – well, the training at least. Chris Pyatt was the special one in the ring. I mean, we could all dance in the ring, do the Ali shuffle, dodge punches with our arms by our side, like the great Herol 'Bomber' Graham, but Chris – who we called 'Boo' – could not only hit hard, but he could take a whacking punch too. He became an ABA amateur champion, a British, Commonwealth and European champion and a three-time world title challenger, and even won a world middleweight title belt, albeit one of the dodgy ones, but he was a world champion, nonetheless. He was a great boxer. I would often go and see him fight because we were very tight in the early days. I'd watch him as an amateur all over the country, and then we had a punch-up of our own.

We were always hustling one another, playing cards, mainly three-card brag, and hanging out at Willie Thorne's snooker hall and another joint around the corner that was seedier but cheaper. One afternoon, I was playing snooker with Boo and his older brother, Raymond, and we had a dispute about a ball or a shot or something. Chris snapped, turned around and said, 'OK, let's fight about it.' By now, he was a junior amateur champion but I was a year older, so I was supposed to be the bigger, stronger one. But he was a champion boxer, for Christ's sake! I thought, *I'm not going to win this fight against a champion boxer, especially with his brother standing there.* I thought about it for a second, put my cue down and then, WHACK! I hit him as hard as I could. My usual operandi: hit first, hit big, you usually win. No! I met him flush in the eye but he barely flinched. So, obviously I knew I was in trouble. It didn't happen there and then as I just ran out the place. But later, he came round to my house and I thought I'd better take this beating, so we had a little scuffle. I took a few whacks and then that was it. But we were never tight again. Ever. We would nod to each other in the street but that was it. I admire Boo for what he achieved in his boxing career. And I treasure the years of fun we had before the fight.

Sport played a big part in who I was at school. I loved the competition, the personal challenge, the tension of sport. In my first year at Ellis, we went to our first athletics meet. I remember being on the coach not saying a word, dry-mouthed and heart pounding. As we stood on the start line for the 100 metres, I could barely breathe. But when the gun went, pow, I was gone, finishing first by a long stretch. I went back to Ellis the next day and I was crowned the hero of the school. For a kid wanting to belong, it was the best.

But then there's another aspect of school, which is socially belonging. Sport gave me a way of expressing myself and getting attention, especially as I liked the girls! But it was otherwise challenging for me. Like in most schools, there was an in-crowd that most people wanted to be a part of. And that's tough when you're not because at that age you're always wanting to belong. The cool girls, the ones we all fancied, were literally the girls with the blond hair and the blue eyes. And more often than not, the boys they went out with had blond hair and blue eyes too . . . Yes, it really was that clichéd. Although, looking back, most blondes were dyed blondes.

At one point, when I was a bit older, I had a girlfriend, or semi-girlfriend, named Mandy Chesney. I found out many years later that her father had told her, 'If you go out with Simon, I will beat you.' It saddened me to hear it, even years later, because I really liked Mandy.

When I was in primary school, I was in the top set at all subjects – I think I was pretty bright. But that all fell apart because there was no driving force at secondary school other than sport, girls, wanting to be part of a group and the acute need to belong. Ellis secondary school, to me, was primarily a playground, a social club. That was it. Yes, we went to class, but I was always late for school. And I was the class clown. I'd walk into the classroom after everyone had sat down and immediately start performing an elaborate excuse about some drama that had happened on the bus. 'Simon, Simon, just sit down, it's OK. It's OK. I've heard the stories twenty times. Just sit down,' the teacher would say in a resigned tone. If you went to school and there was no trouble, you never got suspended or expelled, you were fine. But regarding academic high achieving, expectations weren't the highest, for most of us at least.

So, school was sport and girls – we dreamed about the likes of Diane Cracknel and her sidekick, Linda Ross – and it was hustling with my friends. We gave very little thought to our grades or to qualifications. We gave a lot of thought to dancing and clubbing. We used to go to funk all-dayers all over the Midlands – Nottingham, Derby, Kettering. We'd wear these ridiculous big baggy trousers and dance all day. Upstairs, you'd have funk music and downstairs, it'd be Northern Soul. We were already the kings of sneaking in the cinema and we gleefully applied our skills to the music venues every time a big concert came to Leicester. We'd climb on the roof of De Montford Hall. I drove past there the other day and I thought how the blue blazes did these thirteen-year-old kids scale up this wall into a side window, but we did it every week. I saw some of the biggest acts of the day, including The Jackson 5.

Those years are a blur, like a dream, but sometimes, also like a nightmare.

* * *

When I was fourteen or fifteen years old, I came home from school and Mum was in the lounge, crying.

'He's dead. Your dad . . . Dan. He's dead.'

He'd had a heart attack.

At first, it was just hugely shocking. Then I felt bitterly sad because I didn't really know him. I just didn't know him. We'd barely ever had a real conversation. It dawned on me that I'd lived with my father – this quiet, good, hard-working man – for over ten years and in that time we'd chitter, we'd chatter, but we never had a deep conversation. And then he was gone. He never, ever spoke about his feelings. He never spoke about his Irish history, beyond the 'weak and the wicked'. To this day, there is so much I don't know about him. I didn't realise how much it would hit me. Being so young and detached from him in many ways, his death was another edging towards my realisation that I was on my own. It was down to me. It made me sad, a little bit more vulnerable but also a little more stronger.

I missed Dan very badly, but I was hardly alone in having suffered loss. There was plenty of hardship to go around. I was surrounded by kids who were dealing with one form of trauma or another. Divorced parents, brutal dads. Most of my friends' dads gave their sons 'the belt', or a whack across the face. Many kids were dealing with something, but that was par for the course.

Even those of us who had so far avoided any tragedy or serious deprivation had to find some sort of compass for navigating the big wide world, and we had to find it by ourselves and we had to find it quick. There were plenty of wrong turns, of traps to fall into through youth or stupidity or wanting to belong that you could spend a lifetime failing to get back out of. Even if your parents were around, they most likely simply didn't have the time to help.

Dan's death had made me understand that the world never stands still, that it's constantly shifting. That unspoken, quiet stability he had always provided for me was no longer there. How was I going to navigate this new world of constant change, and where was my place in it?

CHAPTER 3

BOY TO MAN

As a young kid you could say that I was reasonably well read. Not in the traditional sense. There wasn't a bookshelf full of the classics at our home, in fact there wasn't a bookshelf. Although in saying that, my mum would send me and my brother to the library once a week to get three books, novels, with large letters to aid her failing eyesight, which she would then devour. Her love of books never rubbed off on either of us at the time. But eventually it would. No, my worldview came from two sources: tabloids and TV. I got to read the tabloids because I delivered, I'm guessing, thousands of them. When I was about nine or ten years old, I worked for Jimmy Walsh. He had a newspaper shop on Wharf Street, next to Mr and Mrs Hennessy's fish and chip shop, the one we'd go into and ask: 'Mrs Hennessy, have you any cod left?' And she'd reply yes, to which we'd reply with great mirth: 'It's your own fault for cooking too many.' 'Out of my shop, you've wasted my time,' she'd mutter.

Anyway, back to the paper round. I'd arrive at 6am on my bike, sitting on the piles of papers the vans had left. Then Jimmy would turn up. 'Come on, Simon,' he'd say in a Scottish accent, 'let's get this show on the road,' and strong as an ox, he'd lift the piles of papers on the counter, pull out his pen knife, cut the string and start putting the papers in my sack. I could barely balance with my back laden with papers, but the more I delivered, the lighter it got. If I worked quickly, I'd allow myself to read the sport pages. When I was all done, I'd drop the papers back off, chat a little more about football with Jimmy, who seemed to know a lot, and then it was back home to get ready for school. Turned out that Jimmy was more than knowledgeable about football, he was an ex-pro. One morning, I came in and he said: 'Come here, got something to show you,' and from his inside jacket pocket he pulled out a felt case with a medal inside. It was his FA Cup final medal, from 1961. Jimmy, who I viewed as an old man – he must have been all of forty – was a top, top striker, both for Leicester and Celtic. After that, when he spoke about football, I really listened.

So the sports pages, the occasional front-page tabloid headlines, and the BBC News were my global window to the world. It was probably the BBC News that piqued my interest in Vietnam, a lush green place that I only ever knew about because of the war. During one TV news report, my head went into a tailspin when the reporter, in a clipped, matter-of-fact manner, stated, 'Today, twenty bodies were found after a skirmish between American forces and the Viet Cong.' Being young and naïve, my understanding was that a 'body' meant a 'torso'. So, when they said on the news that twenty bodies had been found . . . I was shocked and frightened that all these headless, legless torsos had been discovered. I never asked Mum or Dad about it. I just felt, *oh gosh, how dreadful can this war be that they're hacking heads off and only leaving the body? So that's why those bastard skinheads want to send me to that god-forsaken place! Well, they can go fuck off.*

The other place that loomed large as hell on earth, courtesy of the TV news, was Biafra, a place that became a byword for starvation, famine and bloody civil war. From 1967 to 1970, war raged in Nigeria, resulting in over a million, mainly civilian casualties, widespread hunger and a refugee crisis. Mum would say, 'Finish up your dinner because there are children starving in Biafra.' 'Yeah, well, give it to them,' us kids would think but dare not say.

But it wasn't just the terrible events in Southeast Asia and West Africa that we were aware of, going on in the world. In 1970, I was utterly transfixed by the football World Cup in Mexico. Brazil beat Italy 4–1 in the final and revolutionised the way the 'beautiful game' would be played. I wanted to be Pele just as much as later I wanted to be Muhammad Ali after watching 'The Rumble in the Jungle' between 'the Greatest' and George Foreman in 1974 in Zaire.

Football and Pele, boxing and Muhammad Ali, the Vietnam War and mutilation. These events were the backdrop to a childhood and adolescence within our own concrete jungle, where we made our own fun and earned our money, one way or another. But world events came to Leicester and impacted our lives in a more significant way in the early 1970s, teaching me a lot about belonging, tribes, hatred and where I stood.

In the 1970s, Britain was still coming to terms with the fallout of the Second World War and, particularly, the wide-reaching implications of its crumbling colonial project. At the same time, this was an era in which African leaders were emerging from independence with the desire to recalibrate their countries and forge a post-imperialist future for themselves. The results of this African revolution, however, were often far from progressive.

In East Africa, Idi Amin seized power in a military coup from Milton Obote, Uganda's first prime minister and president following the country's independence. The following year, 1972, Amin announced that the sizeable population of Asian Ugandans had ninety days to leave the country. Many were British citizens and so entitled to seek refuge in the UK. Leicester City Council launched a campaign to dissuade potential refugees from migrating to the city by taking out an advert in the Ugandan press informing them there were no council houses, the schools were full and healthcare provision already overstretched. Yet far from deterring migrants, the advert had the opposite effect and made more Asians aware of the possibility of settling in Leicester. As a result, between 5,000 and 6,000 (nearly a quarter of the UK's first wave of Ugandan refugees) put down roots in Leicester. By the end of the 1970s, another quarter had settled in the city.

There had been a burgeoning Caribbean community in Leicester since the end of the Second World War, typically working on the buses, the railways, factories and – like my birth mother – in the NHS. The Caribbean community was still experiencing dreadful racism in the UK in the 1970s, despite having been in the country, in mass immigration terms, for three decades (though of course, Black people from the Caribbean and elsewhere had lived in Britain for many centuries). Then along came this new wave of migration in the 1970s from Africa: Gujarati Ugandans and Kenyans and the heat – to an extent, and for a while – was finally taken off Britain's Black population. The far right, Powellites, reactionaries and racists on all sides of the political and social divide now had a new folk devil to focus their vitriol on.

My initial personal experience of this was at school, when I heard white friends say, 'The P.... are coming over.' It's a shocking, pejorative phrase but one I used to hear all the time. They were even more explicit, stating, 'Simon, you're not like them because you don't smell like them, you don't eat their food, you don't speak their language, you've not got the same religion as them.' They were the 'them' and we were the 'us'. I'm ashamed to say that as an eleven-year-old, I bought into this 'casual' racism because, ultimately, I wanted to belong: I wanted to fit in.

Jewish friends tell me how it was much the same for their parents' generation. When people came to Britain from the Caribbean after the war, the 'West Indians' took some of the heat off the Jews, giving their community 'a pass', which may well have allowed them to integrate and assimilate in a way they had previously been unable to do. Likewise, the arrival of large numbers of Asian immigrants took a little bit of heat off us Black kids. It was a classic folk devil move: by putting one group down, Black kids could elevate their own status within the social structure and lessen the pressure we were previously under. But our 'pass' came at a price. White kids, informally and formally, now asked and expected us to choose which side we were on.

By the time I'd moved up to Ellis Boys' School in the early 1970s, Asians had started coming to Leicester in much greater numbers. When I was about twelve years old, I found myself caught up in my first mass brawl. It was at a fairground just off the Belgrave Road. A massive fight kicked off between a gang of white kids and a group of Asian lads. Those first fights were not necessarily race fights – everyone against the Asians, although I'm sure that some of them were – they were more turf fights. I was aligned with the white kids; everyone was piling into everyone else, punching, kicking, wrestling to the ground, spitting, swearing. Somebody threw a punch at me; I threw a punch at somebody else. Then, in the melee, I saw the flash of a blade against the night sky. I jockeyed my way through the crowd, moving instinctively away from this new danger towards another section of the ruckus. But when the dust settled, I learned that one of the English kids had been stabbed. In fact, he'd been cut so badly that he needed emergency medical attention. Thankfully, he lived and I went with a group of mates to see him in the hospital. But several things happened in the chaos of that moment that made me realise how racial tensions on the streets of Leicester and beyond were truly getting out of hand.

I was also acutely aware that if my Black friends – the Pyatt brothers in particular – weren't careful, we could wind up in serious trouble with the law, or seriously injured, or worse. It was also obvious that, regardless of whatever many whites had to say about East African immigration, and whatever 'beef' us Black kids thought we had with the Asians, we were on the wrong side. So, the Black experience in Leicester, my experience, became one of occupying the middle ground. I would no longer be blindly on the side of the white gang. I realised that today it was the Asians but the skinheads hated us Black kids too. I also came to admire the Asian kids' resilience. They had been beaten up time and time again, but now they were fighting back.

I was particularly impressed with a group of Asians at my school and the surrounding area, who were part of or affiliated to Satna gang – I later learned that 'Satna' meant the 'Dream'. The dream boys, you couldn't make up. I knew Salesh, who was a few years older than me, big and fearless. He and his pals took on the skinheads and vowed to protect their community.

Some years before the fairground stabbing, I'd seen a

gang of skinheads attack an old Sikh man on St Matthew's estate. Black and Asian youths were genuinely fearful of skinheads. I must have been eight or nine years of age and was walking through the estate when I saw these animals laying into the Sikh guy, beating him to the ground. I watched with sheer horror as he sat slumped on the floor, blood dripping from his turban. I didn't stick around.

* * *

I left Ellis Boys' Secondary comprehensive school in 1977 with CSEs in English, maths, woodwork, metalwork (remember that?), history and geography. But no A-levels, and sixth form didn't exist. You left school and you went to work. You never thought about university; that was never even mentioned by anyone. Going to university, for my generation, for my class, was not even a pipedream. You were lucky to leave school and go into an apprenticeship: girls became hairdressers, boys got a trade. That was the greatest aspiration a working-class lad in Leicester like me could have – to serve an apprenticeship in one of the trades. On paper, at best, I was destined for a life of getting by, but at worst, as a Black teenager coming up in the 1970s, far worst fates could lay ahead.

But by the time I'd reached fourteen or fifteen, I was an adult. I could earn money; I could look after myself. I was ready for the world. Or at least, I thought I was. Mum had given me the confidence to be bold and brave in the face of the big bad world.

I wasn't given any career advice and pretty much left to make my own way. I liked cars, so I applied to my local garage, Latham's, to become an apprentice mechanic. Latham's specialised in British Leyland cars and was literally down at the back of Wharf Street. Lo and behold, I got a three-year apprenticeship. Back then, apprenticeships were proper apprenticeships, City and Guilds and all that, you learned the trade, on the job, the trade of being a car mechanic. I also had to go to college to learn the theoretical side of the job and take exams, so it was a proper three-year investment. Meanwhile, both Chris Pyatt and Savvas became hairdressers. Chris of course went on to box, but Savvas stuck with the hairdressing, right up to this day. Back then, hairdressing was sort of cool, the likes of Vidal Sassoon made it cool for the lads to get into. But me, I became a mechanic.

On the first day at Latham's, which was near Belgrave Road, a predominantly Asian area of Leicester, I walked into the garage, gingerly scanning my new surroundings. There were literally Indian and Pakistani workers on one side and on the other side were white workers and not a single Black employee. The question was, where did I belong? Well, because there were other apprentices, who were white, of course, I stayed with the apprentices. The foreman in charge assigned me to a mechanic named Bob. He was a nice guy, no-nonsense, and thus I set about my new world as a car mechanic earning the princely sum of £15 a week, of which I gave £5 to my mother for food and board. That's what you did – you paid your way.

There were two other apprentices in my year and two others a little bit older. They were often full of it, mucking around if you like. Part of that mucking around was driving cars. Most of them knew how to drive but I'd never driven a motor before; after all, I was only sixteen. One day, they were onto me, telling me they'd teach me how to drive, coaxing me to drive one of the cars in the garage. I said, pumping myself up, 'Yeah, I can do it. I can do it,' and I got into an Austin Allegro that was parked on a slope in the garage. So, there I was in the car, and they were shouting, 'Get off the bloody clutch, get off the clutch!' But my foot was on the accelerator, I was revving. . . and then, I panicked. The car reversed and smashed into the garage wall. Oh my God! I was fortunate as one of the other apprentices had been lolling around behind the vehicle but then suddenly jumped out of the way.

The car wasn't a write-off but it was a godawful mess. I thought, *that's it, I'm going to get the sack.* Honestly, I thought that would be that, I was out. The guy in charge of the apprentices, a fella named Martin, called me into the office. 'You're a dumb fool,' he shouted. 'You're a bloody fool. But I like you, you're a good kid. So we're going to give you a second chance. But you've got to keep away from trouble.'

And with that, one of the Asian mechanics pulled me aside and said, shaking his head, 'Simon, if you want to be a car mechanic, learn this trade properly. Bring your toolkit and come over to the other side, our side.' And so I was put with this guy called Taco, Taco Bhai, 'bhai' meaning brother in Hindi. And I learned my trade with him and then another guy named Jerri, who we also called Jeddy Bhai. It was great.

The Asian mechanics were serious blokes. They knew that they'd never get given the easiest jobs, which you could do the quickest and earn over time. Usually, they'd get the trickiest, most demanding tasks, such as automatic gearboxes, whereas the white mechanics would get the easy ones. So the Asians knew that they had to be better than the white guys to earn the money they needed to.

Not only did I learn loads from Taco and Jerri and the others about being a car mechanic, I was also invited into their culture. So at lunchtime, instead of mucking around like the white boys did, I would sit with the Asian mechanics and they'd produce these tins full of food stacked one on top of the another called dabbas. Typically, the dabbas would contain rice, chapattis, curry and such-like, and we would sit cross-legged in a circle eating the food and shooting the breeze. Being with them was a special time in my life. I learned loads of swear words and Hindi songs because, at that time, Bollywood was just booming in the UK, particularly in Leicester on the Belgrave Road, or the 'Golden Mile' as it had become known. There was the first cinema dedicated to Bollywood films and people would queue up around the corner to get in. I remember singing with my friend Jerri, who was young at heart despite being a lot older than me. He would teach me the Hindustani songs from the movies, I'd sing them badly and we'd crack up laughing together.

The foreman would come around and ask, 'How you doing, Jerri? How's it going?'

'It's very fine, sir,' Jerri would always say, smiling. 'Very good,' before saying under his breath as the foreman walked away, 'doria mara chewce,' which meant 'White bastard, always giving us bad jobs.' And then we'd start laughing together.

Everybody knew the hierarchy. Everybody knew that the set-up in the garage wasn't fair but I just got on with it, and so did everyone else. Nevertheless, whether it was simply the joy of youth or the thrill of new experiences, I enjoyed everything from the food to the culture to learning to be a mechanic. Of course, my white colleagues envied me because I was learning quicker than them.

There were some other things I quickly recognised, aside from the parts of an engine. My first experience of the working world taught me to know my 'place' in society. For example, if someone came in with a new car, they were almost undoubtedly middle class. So you'd stand there polishing the vehicle for them, not in any great shakes, but to show them that you 'cared' about their car. This was obscene, but the fancier the car, the more pride you took in making sure it looked the part. For instance, the Vanden Plas Princess automatic got the full treatment. Bizarre, really.

Essentially, for most of the day, you were on your back covered in grease. When I went into college, I'd be in my grubby overalls, feeling self-conscious, uncharacteristically insecure, even ashamed, even though the other guys seemed happy to go to the cafeteria in their overalls. I would spend fifteen minutes of my forty-five-minute lunch break scrubbing myself and digging the dirt and grease from under my nails until they almost bled. Then I'd peel off those filthy overalls, making sure that no muck marked my 'this is who I really am' clobber, before going into college pretending I wasn't a car mechanic – or at least, not the sort of car mechanic who smells of oil and gets their fingernails dirty. In the end I realised I didn't like getting dirty and having to scrub my hands raw to clean them. The funny thing is now, people at times comment, 'You have soft hands, Simon'. *Yeah*, I think, *that's because I gave up being a car mechanic.* I think the other thing that made me realise the life of a car mechanic wasn't for me – although I didn't acutely know it at the time – was that, at that time, being on the first rung of the ladder was not like being in an F1 garage with Lewis Hamilton. I felt subservient, slightly looked down upon. And I know that's more about my insecurities at the time than the real skill of any car mechanic. But I had to deal with me, and where I was or wanted to be in the world. I think I felt there might be more to my life, that I could do a bit better.

I did at least manage to buy my first car during this period, a MINI Clubman, which I jazzed up with a small sports steering wheel. There were no furry dice – I was too cool for that – but I had almost every little trinket that you could have in or on the car. Including the obligatory cassette player – stolen several times – in-built speakers, wheel trims and lovingly polished and expertly, mechanically taken care of by yours truly.

* * *

I was still knocking around with Savvas and I now also had some other friends who were a bit more middle class. There was Graham Smith: he was a teacher; then there was Martin Tolly, who ran a guesthouse for his father, where we'd go for drinks. The world that Graham and Martin lived in was a million miles from me and Sav. They were both university graduates, they were older, and back then, both drove what we perceived to be the coolest car on the planet, the VW convertible. It was, still is, the type of car you don't have to drive fast in to be cool. In fact, the slower the better. So I felt that I was starting to arrive, hanging out with these guys.

One day I met these guys who came from London, who were staying in the guesthouse. They were shower salesmen who were up in Leicester expanding their calling ground. They were fast-talking, smart, owned sports cars and they always dressed sharp. One evening, we were drinking together and they said they were looking to recruit new salesmen. By this point, I'd been in my job for three years and had just about finished my apprenticeship. And I thought to myself, *Hmm . . . this is interesting*. One of them said, 'Look, we're going to do a little bit of work in Leicester for a couple of weeks. Why don't you come and join us and see what you think?' I agreed and then went to my boss and said, 'I'm taking a couple of weeks off.' I joined these salesmen and went canvassing door-to-door as part of a group of ten, getting leads that the salesmen would then follow up on. I must have been a proper picture given that I didn't have any formal work shirts, which were not needed in the garage, of course! So the only shirts I had were my disco shirts that I'd bought from Paul Smith in Nottingham. Trouble was they were either bright yellow or sparkly black – you get the picture.

It didn't matter because something clicked in my brain; it was just like ticket touting or bob-a-job – I had to get the most leads for the salesmen. I knew the drill; it's a numbers game, and I was hungry for those numbers.

So, at the end of the two weeks, the Londoners said to five of us, 'We want you to come and join us as part of our central London team,' which really meant Redbridge, Essex.

I'd barely been out of Leicester. I'd been to a few gigs and clubs in places like Nottingham and Coventry and the odd away match watching Leicester City. I'd been to London a few times shopping. And that was it. The sales team proposed that I leave home and go to London to work.

I can't remember the conversation I had with Mum about it, but she accepted my decision. We'd decided that it would be a very short-term move – six months to a year, maximum, and then I'd come home. And so I went to London. Extraordinarily, I just did it. I packed some clothes, jumped in my little MINI Clubman and, like Dick

Whittington, I headed to the capital. The salesmen put me up in a bedsit in South Woodford on the border of East London and Essex. (Funnily enough, the second flat I would end up buying was just one hundred yards from that first bedsit. I was nineteen years old. Now I'm sixty, and I've lived in the same area that whole time, for forty years. Well, now I also live in Cambridge, but we'll come to that later. I started off at the end of the street, and now I'm further up with one or two moves in between. It's incredible.)

The bedsit was horrible, a right dump. After two weeks, three of the five people who came down to London from Leicester went back, homesick. A young woman named Brenda and I stayed. The funny thing is, she was also an adopted, or maybe fostered, child. The top salesman was a guy called Steven Skolnick. He was a fast-talking, sharp-suited, funny, sports-car-driving, super salesman. He could charm the birds from the trees. He said to me, 'Listen, Simon, you're too cool to stay in a shitty little bedsit. Come and live with me. Come and rent a room with me.' He owned a house in Chadwell Heath, Essex, where he lived with Johnny Montlake. Johnny Montlake was the son of a High Court judge and smoked joints all day. He didn't work, just smoked joints and listened to the blues and Van Morrison. That was his gig: just chill out, smoke joints and be cool.

So, I went from a crummy bedsit to a suburban house with this guy, Skolnick, and thus, by default, became ensconced in the Essex Jewish community. The firm's boss, Ian Charles, was Jewish, most of the workers were Jewish and then there was me, a young Black kid from Leicester. Talk about fish out of water. But they, Steven, Ian and others went out of their way to make me feel welcome.

I quickly transitioned from canvasser to salesman, selling showers door-to-door. When canvassing, you'd get the lead and say to a potential customer, 'Would you like to save a whole heap of money on your weekly budget? Er, yes! We're in the area for the shortest time, but if you really want to save a whole heap of money, and literally, as my boss reminds us, be the cleanest family in the street, then I'll send a salesman round to talk you through what our wonderful showers can do; blah, blah, blah.' But as a salesman, you had to be tough; it was a hustle, really, selling showers. You had to use every trick in the book, bend the rules to almost breaking point because no sale meant no money. And no money, to me at that time, meant that I couldn't become the person I wanted to be, with the sharp suit and flash car.

One of the sure-fire tricks that we used was the reverse pitch – give them the wonders of the shower, its savings, its cleanliness, and then abruptly take it away. So we'd go into a house and give the spiel about all its benefits, at which point they were halfway there. And then you'd say to the family, 'Ah, I should have started with this because I could be wasting everyone's time. We've been alerted that this is a low water pressure area and not everyone can have our state-of-the-art showers.' Most households often struggle with water pressure, so most nodded, 'Yeah, we know about that.' 'OK,' I'd say, 'let's check.' We'd go upstairs to the bathroom, where I knew the water pressure would be low, saying, 'I'm sure it's going to be fine but let me just see . . .' Then we'd turn on the hot and cold water. And the usual lack of robust flow spoke volumes, particularly my practised look of despair. 'I'm sorry. I'm sorry, but with this level of pressure we simply can't fit your shower.' I'd zip up my sales case and say, 'I should have started here, not wasted your time,' and they'd be like, 'Are you sure we can't have one? I know my neighbours, John and Jenny, have one.' 'It's house by house, I'm afraid, this water pressure malarkey. I can't tell you how disappointed I am for you.'

I'd slowly walk down the stairs, ready for act two of my sales drama, listening to them lament about what they couldn't have, then say, 'Give me just one second. Let me just check downstairs because sometimes there's another feed and the pressure is so much better. Then we could take it from that. I can't promise anything but let me check.' I'd know all along that that was the main feed. So I'd walk into the kitchen, turn on the cold water and the water would start gushing out. I'd turn to them with a smile and wait until they spoke first. 'Simon,' – we're now on first-name terms – 'does this mean we can have one of your showers?' 'It certainly does, my dear. Shall we go to the lounge?'

It's still not quite a done deal, but we're close. I'd once again open my black zipped booklet, pull out a selection of coloured shower curtain samples, and, in those sexist times, I'd turn to the female member of the household and politely ask, 'Sarah, what colour curtains would you like?' And as quick as a flash, she'd reply, 'Hmm . . . pink' or 'I like the blue . . .' And while she was browsing through the samples, I'd, almost with a sleight of hand gesture, get out a contract, turn to the husband (well, it *was* the late seventies), and ask, 'Dave, would you like to pay cash or terms?' Knowing full well it was always terms.

The deal was done. As I write, I know I'm making it sound relatively easy. It wasn't. Sometimes you could be in and out in thirty minutes, deal done. Other times it was a war of attrition until they signed. Most times you came away empty-handed. There were a lot of lessons I learned about work during those years. Some were sales quotes, but relevant: Every no you get means you're nearer to a yes; and when the going gets tough, the tough get going. Above all, I got to know people, in their personal homes; their likes and dislikes, their hopes and dreams for their families. How they viewed the world from their perspective.

I was also thrust into another world, a secular Jewish world. One Friday, my boss Ian invited me round to his house for Shabbat dinner, which was a big deal. His house was amazing – he even had a pool and drove an open-top two-seater Mercedes with the number plate 'Ian 2' or something. I'd never seen anything like it. He said to me during the meal, 'Simon, you're doing brilliantly. You're one of our top salesmen. I'm really, really pleased with your performance. So how do you like it in London?'

At this point, I'd not long moved out of Skolnick's place

into another fella's house in nearby Woodford. He was a piece of work.

'Yeah, it's fine,' I replied. 'But the guy I live with is a right Jew.'

Everything stopped. The world as I knew it froze, you know like one of those scenes in the movie, and there's just me in motion: fuck, fuck, fuck. What did I just say in front of a Jewish family? Are you completely stupid, Simon? Then the freeze frame stopped. Everyone around the table put down their cutlery and looked around. What I'd meant to say was the guy was incredibly mean. What had I done? I was just a kid from Leicester who had never knowingly met a Jewish person before I moved to London, just a few months previously. In my psyche, my psyche of racist Britain, 'a Jew' meant a stingy or tight-fisted person. You'd say to your friends at school, 'Don't be a Jew, give me a sweet.' And there it was, laid bare. I could have died. It was shocking. Of course, I apologised profusely. Fantastically, when everyone at the dinner table had listened to the whole story and saw how sorry I was, they said, 'Look, we get it, Simon. We get it. It's not nice, but we get it. You're a kid, Simon, but please, no more.' I wanted to cry, not because of what I'd said, but because Ian and his wife Jackie were so quick to forgive me.

Of course, this incident helped bring about a sea change in my thinking. I didn't realise it then, but I do now. It taught me a lot about the politics of race, particularly around jokes, jibes and stereotypes.

* * *

You know life's journey is full of twist and turns; side roads, cul-de-sac magical roads that you don't really know where they end. Often the trick is to see those roads that offer at least an opportunity.

And there it was for me while up in the West End on a date. I was taking a girlfriend to see Andrew Lloyd Webber's *Evita* at the Prince Edward Theatre.

By this time I'd graduated from selling showers to fresh coffee vending machines for offices in the West End, and now I was selling the cheap wonderful tacky ads you used to see at the cinema for Rank Films. You know the one: stock film of a couple entering an Indian restaurant, with a voiceover: 'Come to the best Indian restaurant in town', and then a picture of their restaurant would be on the screen. Anyway, that was my new job, and I'd earned enough to take my new girlfriend to a show, to impress her. We were standing in line to go in and a ticket tout appeared. 'Tickets, tickets. Anyone looking for best tickets? I buy or sell. Tickets . . .' I watched as the tout spotted an American tourist.

'Ticket, sir? Over from the States, don't tell me, sir, New Yorker, right? Am I right?'

The flattered American man replied, 'Yes, you're a hundred per cent correct. How did you know?' 'Sir, you look a million dollars and your wife ten million. And I've got good seats for you, sir. They're £40 each.'

That was big money then but the man got out a bundle of notes, and I mean a proper bundle, and started to count them out. Quick as a flash, the tout cut in, 'Sir, just so you know, I have only two of the very best tickets in the house I was holding back for a customer who's already late. If you'd really like to impress,' nodding to the man's wife, 'these are the tickets you need, or I can give you the cheaper seats…?'

The American was duly charmed and relieved of £160, for which two minutes earlier the tout would have gladly accepted £80.

And I thought, *I want some of that.* This touting, albeit in London's West End, was something I knew a little about.

So the next week, I was there. Then I went to stand outside *Les Misérables,* 'Les Mis', as we fondly called it. I kept thinking, I've worked a number of years outside the ground at Filbert Street and I thought I could do the same thing here. Of course, now I'm not in Leicester on my own turf, I'm in London's West End, and this, by and large, belonged to the cockneys. No surprise then that within a week or so, just as I was getting to know the ropes, this big fella came up to me and said, 'Whatever you're doing here, make this your last day. I don't want to see you here again.' But the next week I went back, got the same hostility, but just kept coming back. There were a few stand offs, but I somehow managed to hold my ground, and in the end was accepted by most of the touts who came from all parts of London, predominantly the South – the Bermondsey Boys, the East End and North London.

I had to learn quickly, particularly the vernacular – the street language – which was for me a hybrid of cockney back slang and rhyming slang, for example, 'an apple' …. Carpt cching. Gavers on the hay stack – police behind you. Nevis seven, rofe… etc., and Yiddish, because of my colleagues and friends in Redbridge – Gants hill, Smichi, Yoke, gentle, and me of course the yiddisar swarsa, The Black Jew. But the real essence of belonging in that world was being good at what you did. It was just like being in a parallel universe. There was a world where normal people went to do a 9 to 5 working week, and earned enough to get by and there was this other world where you'd work the weekend and earn enough for the whole week, often a lot more.

These guys taught me a lot; how to be sharp, how to read someone in a few seconds, how to see an opportunity. Back in the 1980s, you could earn serious money doing this, maybe £500 in a day. These guys almost just peeled off notes from big fat wads of cash. It was all about the wad. You'd have a wad of cash and peel off notes – tens, twenties, fifties.

I used the money I earned from it to pay my way through university and get a degree as a mature student. I could pivot from being a street hustler to a graduate, while my fellow touts found it more difficult to break away from street hustles.

That time in the West End taught me one of the great lessons. While talking to customers, weighing up who wants to buy what, I learned to read people. To quickly understand who they are, what they want, whether they're friend or foe. Because you had to have that antenna if you were to get to wherever you wanted to be.

* * *

I was doing my Rank Film job during the week and spivving at the weekend. And then I experienced a moment that was to be life-changing. I've got to rewind a little bit, and the dates might not be exact, but in general this is how I remember things. Soon after working for Rank Films, I think I was twenty-one, I bought my first flat, a first-floor, two-bed place in Waverley Road, Walthamstow. Two things are relevant at this stage; firstly, not everyone was buying flats at this age, but the young guys that I was hanging around with all had their own flats: Gary, Gabby, Skolnick. And secondly, perhaps more importantly, it was the opening up of the financial markets. The old rules of saving for a deposit, then buying a house were gone, not forever, but for a few years banks and credit card companies were throwing money at you. As long as you had a job, and I think the mortgage had a ceiling of twice your salary, the money was yours. I think I was on a basic of £20k plus bonus and so the mortgage that I wanted was £22k. Anyway, in the end I get a 110 per cent mortgage. Yep, you read that right. Not only did I not put a penny towards it, they gave me two grand to move in. Which basically meant I could buy all my furniture.

There was only one small, well, enormous snag. I didn't,

couldn't, tell my mum that her son, of whom she'd said, 'I don't worry about you', had managed to buy his home, not least because in my mind it would have meant that I wasn't coming home. And I couldn't bear saying that.

Then, about six months after I bought my flat, I got a call from back home. My mother, Pippi, had died. She was sixty-three. She had given us a household full of love and a home full of warmth. It's something of a working-class cliché of that era but despite having little in the way of material things, we had each other. Until we didn't.

I was full of grief and disbelief that she was gone. But I was also awash with guilt. Because I had met my birth mother without her knowing.

I was seventeen the first time that I met Lolita. Before that, all I'd ever seen of her was a photo that Pippi showed me of her, in her early twenties. But to me, then, it was just a picture of a woman who was my mother. When you know that you are fostered and adopted, that curiosity, *who is my family?* is unavoidable. I wouldn't say it raged in me but it gnawed at me.

Then one night, when I was seventeen years of age, I went to a nightclub in town – a provincial nightclub for what would have been an otherwise unmemorable night out, except for the fact that something extraordinary happened. Some guy came up to me and told me that my mother wanted to meet me. So we exchanged numbers and we arranged a time for me to visit my mother.

On the appointed day, I went to the house. I remember

there was a lime green BMW parked outside. My mother's car. The door opened. Lolita walked through the door and looked at me. She opened her arms out, beckoning me. I edged forward and she gave me a big hug. My response was . . . well, lovingly awkward. This was my mother, after all.

'I'm sorry,' she said. 'I'm really sorry.'

'It's OK, it's OK. It's fine, it's all good. It's all good.' It wasn't a Hollywood moment, above all because as we let go from that embrace I was overwhelmed by guilt. I felt that I had betrayed my other mother, Pippi. Looking back, I'm sure she would have understood, but when I was twenty-one, grieving my mother's death, guilt at seeing Lolita, of the thought of 'betraying' Pippi, was mixed in with all those other feelings.

I'm guessing like many people who grieve after a big loss, helping to organise the funeral arrangements kept me focused. But I wanted to do more than that. I knew my mum was special and I wanted the whole world to know about it, so I took it upon myself to go to the *Leicester Mercury* and tell them to write an obituary about an extraordinary woman who looked after hundreds of kids. To my amazement they did. And it made me very proud.

It would be many more decades until I got back in touch with my birth mother again, the feeling of betrayal was so deep. It wasn't until the birth of own son, Luca, that rekindled our relationship and allowed mother and son and grandson to have a loving, understanding relationship.

Shortly after my first encounter with my elder brother he

went off to Barbados to live and we lost touch for a number of years.

Most people are lucky if they have one mother who loved them – I've had two. They both come from different continents and different perspectives, but they both love me dearly.

CHAPTER 4

VIVA LA REVOLUCIÓN

W hen I was twenty-one or twenty-two I saw a job in the newspaper for The Rank Organisation – then still an international, renowned, iconic film company. They were looking for salespeople and I decided to go for it. I was a good salesman but still young and relatively inexperienced – on paper, at least; for obvious reasons I didn't mention the ticket touting at my interview! I must have done well at the interview because they liked me and offered me the job. I even got a company car, a Vauxhall Cavalier. I couldn't believe it!

The Rank Organisation was based in Wardour Street, in London's Soho. However, the job was not as glamorous as it sounds. Not that I told anybody that. I'd be sent to various towns and cities around the country, where I'd rock up at the cinema and introduce myself. Then off I'd go, looking around town for local businesses that might be persuaded to advertise before film showings. When you went to see a film at that time, you'd get these big, slick ads from Coca-Cola, the cigarette companies, that sort of thing. But alongside these national ads, there were local ads and that was me. I was expected to come back from each trip with about ten or twelve good leads for potential customers.

Let's say there was a local Indian restaurant. The advert might be some stock footage of, say, the Taj Mahal. Then at the end there would be a photo of the restaurant with some text, reading something like, 'Come to Raj's restaurant on the high street for a true taste of India.' I used to have a folder with stills of these ads that I'd carry around with me. I'd walk into the restaurant, introduce myself and explain that I worked for the big film distributors in London. 'We do the worldwide films,' I'd explain. 'I'm here in Loughborough for one week only, and I want to put you on the big screen. Looking at your restaurant, I can imagine the food. I can see you are a good restaurateur. You need to be on the silver screen. When the lights go down and there's a full house, getting ready to watch John Travolta, they will see you first.' 'What, me?' they'd say. And I said, 'Yeah, you, you!' Which was economical with the truth because it would of course be the name and a photo of the restaurant rather than the person I was talking to. But that was my sell! For four or five years, I went everywhere – up north, down south, to the Midlands. I was a good salesman and it was good money. Within six months, I had bought my own flat.

I visited Oxford and then Cambridge to sell cinema advertising to businesses there. I had never been to those cities before and I was struck by the manicured gardens, the ancient colleges with their porters' lodges, everyone riding bikes with baskets full of books. It was old-fashioned and romantic, and here were all these students – bright young things with even brighter futures. It opened my eyes to something I hadn't known I'd wanted but I was also struck by a powerful sense of inferiority. You could look at it that I had left school without any A-levels and now here I was working for The Rank Organisation as a salesman, with a company car and my own flat. I was doing better than many my age and far better than most from my sort of background. And this was the 1980s, don't forget – the era of the yuppie! But something was missing. I knew I wanted to learn, I was thus determined to get back into education.

I went to my boss and asked if I could do the job part-time because I wanted to study. But he didn't understand at all. He said, 'You need to choose. You're the top salesman, you're going to be a manager. Or you can ditch it and go off on this flight of fancy.'

He had a point. I was twenty-six now and one of his top-earning salesmen. And I'd just told him that what I really wanted to do was a few A-levels. He didn't get it. After all, that's how kids start out. They do well in school so they can get a good job. But I already had a good job and I wasn't a kid anymore, I was an adult.

But I knew that I really wanted to go back to college.

I was good at the hustle, I had been doing the hustle for years. Now I wanted to be someone who studied, who knew things and wasn't only about the smooth chat. So I said to my manager, 'No, I'm done.' I dropped my car keys on his desk and that was it for my career at The Rank Organisation.

I'd learned a lot there and it had given me a lot of financial stability – more than my parents could ever have dreamed of. By the time I left, I had two flats, living in one and letting a friend stay in the other. And I still had the touting in my back pocket to pay the bills, which I had never really stopped, despite the theatre I sold tickets outside at the time being the Palace at Cambridge Circus, which is about three blocks away from Wardour Street. So the executives from Rank could have easily walked by and seen me touting tickets after work. That job was only semi- illegal, of course, and it could stop at any minute. Or I could get bashed up by someone who decided they wanted me off the patch. But it was possible to make £400 or even £500 just on Friday and Saturday, which would get me through college and hopefully uni without too huge a compromise on my lifestyle. It gave me a platform to do something I really wanted to do.

* * *

I went to Epping College on the outer reaches of East London and asked if I could enrol to do A-levels. They explained that as a mature student, I didn't need to sit A-levels; I could instead qualify for higher education by doing something called an 'access course' – a one-year course that Margaret Thatcher had brought in. It was intended for mature students to quite literally learn how to learn. The focus was on exploration, interpretation, analysing, research and generally understanding the art of learning. This was in stark contrast to what I'd been used to at school – mainly reading books just to muddle my way through exams.

There were about ten of us in this class, mostly women in their twenties and thirties. And so we started out again at school. I passed the course and I got a place at Middlesex University, which had a connection with the college. It was particularly welcoming for mature students, which was great for me because, aged twenty-seven, I didn't want to be cast adrift in an academic sea of kids straight out of school, despite my youthful disposition. As mature students, our mission for learning was very different to the eighteen-year-olds: we were learning because we wanted to learn. I wasn't doing it because I thought I had to get a good job, or for the social side, because I wanted to go out and get drunk. For me, it was something of an idealistic dream: I wanted to be a learning person.

The other attraction was that Middlesex offered modular degrees, for which you could just pick and choose subjects and create your own degree, like toppings on a pizza, At the time, I saw myself as a bit of a thinker, so I decided I had to study philosophy. This is what you do, right, to be a real intellectual? Well, no. I took a philosophy class and I couldn't understand a word! So I dropped that and focused on English literature instead. I also chose English language and history. And you had to select a language. I picked Spanish, mainly because I had been to Gran Canaria with my friend Gary and loved it out there. I admired the beautiful, melodic and passionate language and thought a smattering of Spanish would be useful. (Plus, there was a very pretty Spanish au pair who lived down the road from me!) That was really my entire motivation. It's funny how the most seemingly inconsequential decisions can take you down a life-changing path.

I enjoyed Middlesex. It was a fantastic place to study. There were two campuses: one in Enfield and one in Trent Park, where Winston Churchill had occasionally stayed as a guest of Sir Philip Sassoon. It was a grand house and a beautiful place of learning. The history of ideas was excellent. The mature students just threw themselves into it, worrying these ideas like a dog worries a bone.

Learning Spanish at Middlesex allowed me to go abroad to study. My brilliant and inspiring Spanish teacher Francisco Fernandes told me that I could either go to Bilbao, where Middlesex had a connection with the university there, or Costa Rica. I jumped at the opportunity of studying at the University of San José in Costa Rica for a couple of terms, which was the better part of a year. Making a move was a no-brainer: I was adventurous, I could rent out my flat and just go.

Another reason why I was interested in going to Costa Rica rather than Spain was down to my Spanish and Latin

American teacher, who was from Chile. I think he was a refugee. And specifically a book we studied with him: *The Open Veins of Latin America* by Eduardo Galeano. Like lots of students at the time, I was hugely inspired by this book, published in 1971 at the height of the Cold War, and it became like my political bible at the time. It analyses the history and impact of European colonisation on Latin America, including slavery, and lays bare the brutal oppression of capitalist America imposing its will on Latin American countries that wanted socialist government. Studying this book and learning about the politics of Latin America felt hugely important to me and stirred a political side I had only vaguely known I had. A result of this political education was that I learned words and explanations for things I had seen and experienced in my own life but had never had the vocabulary to question or challenge.

I think it would have been hard for anyone who grew up in the 1970s to have been completely oblivious to the politics. As a Black kid, it was certainly impossible for me. When I was about nine, my mother used to send my brother and me to a barber's in an area of Leicester called Highfields. My mother, not being Black, had struggled to know where to find someone who could cut our hair. A friend of hers, Mary, told her we need to go to Barber Joe. So my brother and I would go at around 10 o'clock on a Sunday morning.

It wasn't a commercial barber's shop – just Joe's bedroom. It was a big room with a TV above the bed and a few stools. There'd be one or two people in there and we would sit on the end of his bed and wait. You never said a word. You sat down, kept quiet and waited until Joe and his friend Bob had done most of the adults. That might be until three or four in the afternoon. We'd just sit there and listen to the men talking. They were always dressed beautifully and took great pride in their clothes. No matter how little they had, they demanded to look good, even while getting their hair cut in someone's bedroom. I remember in particular the beautiful crocodile shoes and silk socks. And you could see Joe's party shirt hanging up on the wardrobe.

Because I was brought up in a white family, I couldn't understand patois. I knew the swear words, though, and I could often tell that they were cussing white people and lamenting the state of the countries they were from. Even though much of the Caribbean had gained independence by the late 1960s and early 70s, these countries were still in practice run by white people. In reality, the balance of power had not shifted. The conversation and debate would get very animated and very loud. It was the first time I heard political debate like this. That I saw people who looked like me, who lived where I lived, talking about inequality. As a kid, you don't really know how to process it but it clearly made a big impression as decades later, I still remember it vividly.

'The Rumble in the Jungle' was just before my thirteenth birthday. This was also a very big influence on me – even if I didn't know how to articulate it at the time – because all of a sudden there was Muhammad Ali, the best fighter on the planet, talking so eloquently and passionately about Black empowerment. As a child, you just want to belong to something, to see people who look like you. So the huge amount of Black pride around Ali felt very special. At the same time, I was acutely aware that plenty of white people didn't like Ali because of the colour of his skin and what he stood for.

When I was about thirteen I was made head of the school council. I'd like to think it was because I was already showing early signs of strong leadership qualities, but more likely was that the teachers had decided it might be a good outlet for my big mouth tendencies and desire to be the centre of attention! Well, I can't remember what it was about now but at one point I led the students out on strike. This was the 1970s, an era famous for ongoing industrial action and clashes between miners and the police, so it's not hard to guess where we got the idea of going on strike from! I remember it being quite an intoxicating feeling, the idea that the students could refuse to go to class and in so doing, we could persuade the teachers to listen to our point of view. I think I spoke to the Head, who was happy to hear us out and to try to resolve whatever it was we were unhappy about, but unfortunately most of my comrades were less interested in diplomacy and negotiation and more interested in getting out of their classes, so I think we lost the democratic argument in favour of mob rule on that occasion! It probably only lasted about a day.

Before I went to university, I didn't have much knowledge

of global politics. But learning about the never-ending turmoil in Latin America and the spectre of US imperialism constantly putting its big nose into the region and fuelling uprisings everywhere lit a political fuse inside me. This time studying in Costa Rica would be my very first experience of travelling so far from home, living abroad or surviving by speaking an entirely different language in a radically different culture. And I was intrigued to see this hotbed of radical politics that we'd been studying in class for myself.

* * *

Of course, I soon discovered that Costa Rica was probably the safest country in Central America and not the political cauldron I'd been expecting. In 1990, Guatemala was in a state of civil war; El Salvador was in a state of civil war; Nicaragua was, you guessed it, in a state of civil war. But being in one of the safest and probably calmest countries in the entire Caribbean-Americas region was a wonderful experience.

Every weekend from our base in San José, where we studied at the university, a group of us would head west to Manuel Antonio, a breathtakingly beautiful national park on the Pacific coast, or go eastwards and hang out on the Caribbean coast. It was an amazing experience in so many ways, though in the six months we spent in Costa Rica we partied a lot and, to be honest, we learnt very little Spanish. We found the country to be very US-facing – most people wanted to practise their English with us.

However, while we were staying in San José there was an earthquake. We had experienced little tremors before but this was a full-blown earthquake. The apartment building we lived in shook to the core and in the main town, the buildings were quite badly damaged. It was really quite dramatic. We found out that the epicentre was inland, where the banana plantations were. So, along with some of the other students I knew – being young and idealistic and seeing ourselves as activists – we went to a meeting to see how we could help.

I was told by one of the indigenous leaders that I could go and help in a remote place up in the jungle where they were struggling with little water and no resources. Despite the damage caused in the area, they had somehow got the rickety old train up and running, as it was essential to the banana plantations and therefore a big priority. So off I went, on my own, on the train, through the jungle, up through the rainforest. It was absolutely beautiful but when I got right into the heart of the jungle I could really see the devastation that had been caused. Bridges had fallen down and eventually we had to get off the train and then hack our way through the jungle.

I stayed with an indigenous leader, which was a fascinating experience in itself. What I also found remarkable was that in this remote area in the middle of Costa Rica, living alongside the indigenous Indian families were also people of Caribbean descent, mainly of Jamaican origin. Their ancestors had originally gone there to help build the

American-owned railway to serve the banana plantations in the 1870s and some had decided to stay, mixing with and marrying the locals, living in palm-leaved huts.

I got to see first-hand how this population was treated by big government. In the wake of the earthquake, the government was focused on ensuring that the banana plantation were able to operate, with food and water for the local people a much lower priority. I helped to shift the rubble of some of the houses that had collapsed and was shown such amazing hospitality. It was a beautiful experience and a valuable opportunity to see how the politics of the country played out in reality, how it affected the people who lived there, after reading so many books and studying it back in London. I took lots of notes and wrote them up but I knew that, as a student, there was little I'd be able to do to bring attention to what life was like for these people deep in the interior. Still, it felt good to be helping on the land and showing solidarity in my own small way, and I learnt a lot.

Before heading back to London, along with some of the other students I visited Guatemala and Mexico. I thought that would be it for my adventures in Latin America for a while, but when we got back to Middlesex we were told that the curriculum had changed. It would now be possible to major in Spanish, but it would mean spending a whole other year abroad. Well, I had fallen in love with the region so I jumped at the chance.

* * *

My neighbour in London, Chico, was Colombian. When I started learning Spanish, the pair of us would go to Latin American clubs together. Salsa was a big thing in London in the 1990s. One night we were in some salsa club in the West End.

'So, you like salsa,' Chico said, lining up another round of tequilas.

'Sure, it's great,' I replied.

'And you like beautiful weather. And you want to go to college in South America. You should go to Cali, in Columbia, where I am from, to study. It's the capital of salsa and you can stay with my parents. It's perfect. And you like beautiful women, no? Our women are the most beautiful in the world, *como los flores*, just like flowers.'

It did sound perfect. So I did absolutely no research – the university seemed happy to let me do my own thing this time – and I booked a plane ticket to Cali, in the Valle del Cauca department of southwestern Columbia. If I had done any research at all I would have learnt that Cali was practically the drug capital of the world, second only to Medellin, home to King of Cocaine Pablo Escobar. And I wouldn't have gone. It was what is called a 'narcotic democracy' or a 'narco-state' – a city or area run by the narco *trafficantes* on the power and wealth of the drug trade.

Needless to say, I was pretty naïve. But I arrived in Cali, Chico's family picked me up and they took me back to their place. I had no plan, I just went into the La Universidad del Valle and presented myself and asked if I could study.

They said yes and by the end of my first week I was enrolled to study Latin American literature and I had found a job teaching English. And so began my year-long adventure in Columbia. It was magical and wonderful – and crazy and hardcore.

The sun always shines in Colombia and, just as Chico had promised, there was a real salsa atmosphere – the music played everywhere: on the bus and booming out from all the bars on Friday nights. The sprawling university was a fantastic place. It was very sporty; we played football and I joined the gym and the athletics team, though I noticed that not many of the students gravitated towards me for some reason. And then I realised that the ones that did tended to be the Black students. So there was a racial thing going on – if you were Black, you were a second-class citizen. This carried on for a few weeks but then word got around that I wasn't a Colombian, I was British-African. I went from being ignored by a large part of the Hispanic students to suddenly being an object of interest once they realised I was British. Which for me was just about as hurtful as it could get.

Fortunately, though, by this point, I'd met a group of Colombians I got on with really well. They were sitting around talking literature and politics and asked me to come and join them, introducing me around the group. That first conversation was quite an education for me. After a little while, somebody pulled out a small bag of cocaine. They put some between their thumb and index finger – like how I imagined you might take snuff! Then they casually passed it around. It came to me and I didn't know what to do. I didn't have too many friends and these guys seemed interesting, so after hesitating for a moment, I did it. Gosh, did that conversation flow! And they became my friends.

One of the group, Carlos, was a bit of a junkie – he took cocaine all the time, but still, he was a good guy and became a friend. He took me around to parties and introduced me to people. In fact, I got into trouble once with Carlos and cocaine. We'd gone to the house of one of his friends, the type of old colonial house with a patio garden in the middle. We were sitting around having a few beers, a bite to eat, and this guy arrived and put on the table the biggest bag of cocaine I'd ever seen. The evening was going very well, we were talking about politics and lots of other things, but I decided to take some of the coke. I started to get anxious and eventually completely paranoid. It was like my whole body was convulsing with anxiety. I was convinced that they were plotting to do something horrible, though they weren't. But they could see I was getting into a bit of a state and decided to play up to it for a joke. I was so scared that when they weren't looking, I went to another room and got a knife out and hid it under my sleeve, thinking I would need to protect myself. Then I just ran for the door.

Carlos caught up with me and reassured me that everything was OK and they'd just been joking, but that was me done with cocaine. It really shook me, that feeling I might get killed, but equally what I might have to do if I was attacked. An overpowering sense of fight or flight, and realising I was prepared to do both.

Another friend, Rafael, wasn't a coke user but apparently his father had been in a gang. He'd got out but still had connections. One day, Rafael and I were visiting his family and we went hiking somewhere up into the mountains. We met this guy in a hacienda, who had horses. There were bodyguards there. He put his arm around me and said, 'Simon, Simon, I'm looking for a contact like you in London . . .' I knew exactly what he was talking about and so I said, 'I'm just a teacher, I just teach Spanish,' and managed to get away from there. But the influence of the drug cartels and the FARC, the military wing of the Colombian Communist Party that was funded by the cocaine trade, was everywhere.

I went with Rafa to visit one of his friends, to a party during the Carnaval de Negros y Blancos, which runs from 2–7 January every year. So, we're in a square in San Pedro, which is on the border of Colombia and Ecuador. The square was packed – about a thousand people or more – many were drunk, all were merry. So, everyone's partying, there's a band playing – one of those brass bands that you often see on TV playing out-of-tune music – and then the mayor gave a speech. This is around midnight. The mayor gave a speech – I've drunk far too much. Then I just gravitated towards the stage and got up on the stage, and my Spanish was OK. Still, it wasn't fantastic, but suddenly, I had the drunken confidence to introduce myself to the mayor and then asked to give a speech, and there must have been three or four hundred people all drunk, and they're all Hispanic, there are no Black people there, and I'm on the stage. 'My name is Simon,' I bellowed in Spanish, 'I'm from London, and it gives me the greatest pleasure to be with you. You're such wonderful, warm people. When I go back to London, I will tell everyone that the people of San Pedro are the best in the world!'

With a theatrical flourish, I finished by saying, 'The only thing I have to say is, *¡Que vive San Pedro! ¡Que viva la gente de Aqui!'* – the crowd went wild. They were euphoric – at least that's how it felt at the time! What I do know is that I was literally carried off the stage and held up as some god for about five minutes. My friend had looked on, thinking, *what's he doing? What the … ?* It was at that moment, in that drunken, euphoric, happy moment, that I felt the power to move people with oratory and I liked it. I thought it was so special that you could make people happy, that you could convey warmth and generosity, and that was not so much a drug as a feeling that I might have a little bit of a gift to look people in the eye and tell them something that would make them feel empowered, make them feel special, make them feel wanted. I never forgot that day in San Pedro and that's where I first got the bug for wanting to be a communicator, somebody who could take people along a journey.

Bombs would go off in the centre of Cali but it was crazy, you just learned to live with it. For me, coming from London, it was shocking to see pictures on the front pages of the newspapers of bodies strewn, young kids murdered almost on a daily basis, but the *Caleños* were desensitised to it. One day, I went to change some dollars into the local currency, the Colombian peso. I was waiting patiently in the bank and all of a sudden *pow! pow! pow!* and everybody dived on the floor, even the security guard, so I knew things were bad. I tried to stay as still as possible while looking carefully over to my left. I could see that outside the bank a man had been shot. There was lots of shouting – 'Stay where you are! Stay where you are!'

Eventually people got up, the guy who'd been shot was taken away and I went home to my host family. I was still really shaken and I said, 'This is too much. I think maybe I should go home.' They said, 'But, Simon, you are OK, yes? You're in one piece. This happens in Cali!' So I didn't go home. I stayed in a city that was more alive than anywhere else I'd ever known, where you always felt that they wanted to love you or kill you.

CHAPTER 5

CHARTER 88 AND OPERATION BLACK VOTE

With the real possibility of losing readers, which obviously I don't want to do, heartfelt beliefs will not allow me to downplay my hurt caused by Brexit. There are numerous reasons, including the small, but significant, xenophobic strain that led quite a few people to say to people like me: 'We won the vote so fuck off home!' But another key reason – the effects of which are yet to be fully seen – is our nation walking away from the EU Erasmus programme. I know the UK has now set up its own, but some have likened it to a 'Pound Shop Erasmus programme'.

I, like tens of thousands of other Brits, was a beneficiary of the Erasmus programme, an exchange scheme that was set up in 1987 to allow students to study at universities in countries within the European Union, and I can contest without a shadow of a doubt the experience was not only life-changing, but the personal growth of me as an individual within a shockingly short space of time – eighteen months – cannot be overstated. The Turing Scheme, which replaced it in 2021, is a poor substitute.

If I ever become prime minister – unlikely in the extreme – I would finance a gold-star Erasmus-style programme that would allow all young people to either study or volunteer abroad for at least six months. It would be one of the greatest gifts a nation could give its young men and women. Moreover, the experience, particularly the further you go, affords you the opportunity to glimpse other worlds, other lived experiences so far removed from your own that it cannot help to be transformative.

In many ways my life-changing foreign journey occurred by default. When I started at Middlesex University in 1989, students were obliged to take a beginner's language. I'd recently returned from my best friend Gary's mum's apartment in the city centre of Las Palmas, which was more a local hangout than a tourist trap. There, during crazy New Year's Eve celebrations, we partied with locals. I was hooked on most things Spanish. Back in the UK, I started dating a girl from Madrid, and so when it came to choosing a language, it was only ever going to be Español.

What started off as a selfish endeavour – learn a language to speak to girls – became a wondrous platform for self-discovery, and more than that, a wider world discovery.

To be honest, I had no idea what to expect from my adventures in Latin America, but in many ways it was even more than the informative books I'd read before travelling there, including our Latin American bible, *The Open Veins of Latin* by Eduardo Galeano, and writers like Gabriel García Márquez could not quite do justice to my experiences in Ecuador, El Salvador, Guatemala, Mexico and the mad beauty of Colombia at that time.

Perhaps the biggest wake-up call was the shocking fact that when I was growing up on St Matthew's council estate I had never considered that we were living in relative luxury, in global terms. We may have worn hand-me-downs and liberated a few groceries from the supermarket when money was especially tight, but we could turn on a tap and expect to get hot water, once we'd turned on the immersion heater and waited for about an hour. Flick a switch and be confident a light would come on. In Latin America, I would meet people and live in areas where those luxuries were probably never enjoyed, but even worse, I encountered many who were willing to die for the freedoms we simply take for granted.

So I came back to London and not only finished my undergraduate degree but also completed a master's degree in Hispanic literature – I'd got the bug, badly – at Queen Mary University. Something I would not have even dreamt about, much less done, when I left school and started my apprenticeship, aged sixteen. Something else, something stronger, had moved me in those years of studying and seeing an unjust world, but also a world that we have made. Having had that experience, it's impossible to *un*-experience it. The genie is out of the bottle and for me, the only question was: what is your response?

What I was aware of, perhaps confronting my cowardly self, was the clear fact that it would be unlikely in the extreme that I would disappear at the hands of the authorities for speaking out; that I would be forced to join a guerrilla outfit to fight for justice. I wouldn't even be subject to Jim Crow racist enforcement officers, with batons, water cannons or dogs trained to bite Black people, if I marched for justice. In short, I had no excuse on God's earth not to make a stand. Even if, if I'm honest, I didn't know what that stand would be.

* * *

At that moment and at that time I felt both empowered and privileged on so many levels to have the opportunity to contribute to making my country a fairer place.

Back then – 1995 – the what's-going-in-London magazine, *Time Out*, was essentially the Londoner's bible and not the thin free-sheet it is today. That said, an organisation called Charter 88 placed an ad in there, looking for volunteers to 'Change our world'. So I showed up at the Clerkenwell offices they shared with the *New Statesman* and they took me on.

Charter 88 had been set up in 1988 with the support of leading political, academic and literary figures with the aim of securing political reform. Throughout the 1980s,

Thatcher's minority government had been centralising power in Westminster – taking it away from the unions and local and regional authorities. The founders of Charter 88 believed that as the UK did not have a written constitution that formally enshrined the rights of its citizens, a Bill of Rights was needed to protect our freedoms and ensure they were upheld, no matter who was in government.

When I joined as a volunteer at the beginning of 1995 there were about twenty people working in the organisation, all very switched-on, right-on individuals. The new director was the charismatic Andrew Puddephatt, the former leader of Hackney Council, who seemed to me to be a sharp political operator. Charter 88 was basically a white liberal, democratic reform group, whose supporters mainly came from the middle-class metropolitan Left.

I learned a great deal from Charter 88 and have stayed friends with many wonderful people who were there during my time with the organisation.

The first, and most significant thing that I learned there, which may sound strange to those who know me as an activist, is that in life, in society, you don't have to be a bystander. Before Charter 88 I was probably like most working-class individuals, in as much as politics and its policies were things done to us, often without anyone consulting us, and at times to our extreme detriment. Take, for example, the last fifty years of national legislation, including an especially pernicious one, the Nationality and Borders Bill, going through Parliament as I write this. All of them bar none have been detrimental to people, particularly from the Asian subcontinent, Africa and the Caribbean; diluting rights and citizenship. This pernicious downgrading of British status is also extended to descendants of the aforementioned continents and countries, regardless of the fact that we were born here. Our Britishness has been legally defined as precarious, meaning it can be stripped away, if the Home Secretary wishes to do so.

What Charter 88 taught me was that not only can you fight back against pernicious policy but you can also begin to fight for progressive policies, including those that might offer great opportunity of equality. During this long political journey I have often felt that our ruling class – be it on the left, right or centre – actually likes to maintain the status quo as long as it ebbs and flows between each from time to time.

Charter 88 gave a glimpse into that exclusive power club, but it rarely understood the working class and it absolutely didn't get race inequality beyond 'Free Nelson Mandela'.

And so everything that was to do with race fell on my lap, as the new volunteer, which I had no problem with, except that I'd only just begun going through my own Black political journey, and now I was leading it at Charter 88.

I must confess, I got lucky when it came to finding the right people at the right time to help me with Black political consciousness. They were Herman Ouseley, head of the Commission for Race Equality – he wasn't a Baron or even a Sir then, but he was a wonderful guy. And the other was Lee Jasper. Even back then he was a public figure, a firebrand who took no political prisoners; Lee was a fast-talking, action-packed, Britain's number one political activist. Racial justice campaigner Darcus Howe, by this time, had stepped back to do more writing. Jasper, in contrast, was the front line.

So when Charter 88 launched the 'Public Inquiry', a UK conversation about what the public cared about, I was charged with getting a sense of what Black Britain might expect from a listening government. To get a grasp of what the big issues were from a man tasked with being a voice for Black Britain, I beat a path to Herman Ouseley.

I'm not sure whether or not it was my audacity or his generosity but he accepted my call for an interview with him. You have to bear this in mind: I was a nobody, a volunteer at the bottom rung in the political and activist world. Herman Ouseley, by contrast, was in charge of a big institution with the political clout to speak to practically anyone if he demanded. And yet this quiet, strong man gave his time to me. We had scheduled a thirty-minute interview. He gave me more than an hour, nearer an hour and a half.

When I mentioned political empowerment and democratic reform, mantras of Charter 88, Herman said loftily, 'This is all very well and interesting, but not many Black people are involved with democratic reform, and if Black people aren't registered to vote, political empowerment is a bit hollow.'

Shortly after my interview with Herman, Brent East Labour MP and future London mayor Ken Livingstone and

Left Black activist Lee Jasper broke away from the Anti-Racist Alliance (ARA) to become part of the National Assembly Against Racism (NAAR) – this would have been 1995. As a keen I-need-to-know-everything volunteer, I went to the NAAR launch at the famous York Hall in Bethnal Green in London's East End. It wasn't long before I saw the guy I'd seen on the news, Lee Jasper. I strolled up to him and introduced myself.

'Where are you from, son?' Lee asked in a paternal manner even though there's only a five-year age difference.

'Charter 88,' I replied.

'What?! What?! What's a Black man doing with that lot?' And then quick as a flash, Jasper thought for a second, recalibrated his viewpoint and said, 'Hang on a second – that's not a bad idea. What's your name?'

'Simon,' I now sheepishly replied.

'Democratic reform should be a Black thing, it's just that it isn't. You stay there, brother, and let's make democratic reform work for us too.'

And that was the beginning of what has evolved into a twenty-six-year friendship and professional relationship. Of course, it hasn't always been a walk in the park with Lee, but if there was one person who I'd say was most instrumental in giving me my Black political compass and twelve-cylinder powerhouse energy, it was Lee Jasper.

Lee was also the CEO of the 1990 Trust, an organisation he set up in 1990, as the name suggests, to protect and pioneer the interests of Britain's Black communities. The

Trust's approach was to engage in policy development and articulate the needs of these communities from a Black perspective. While I was working with Charter 88 on their public inquiry, I was also getting involved in the relationship between anti-racism and democratic reform. Lee and I were doing bits and pieces together and we spoke regularly on the phone. Lee's modus operandi was to talent-spot to find people he could bring into the Black movement, then give them huge tasks, so he could quickly find out who would sink and who would swim in the fast-paced environment he created. He was inspiring and demanding, a force of nature. With new ideas for new projects almost every day you had to somehow keep up. But the result was that the people he worked with tended to be steadfast and committed, prepared to go the extra ten miles for Lee and the cause.

In many ways I had the perfect balance which, looking back, I've had for much of my life. In this case the balance was a middle-class ordered white organisation, with its attention to detail and relative professionalism. And on the flip side, Lee Jasper and the 1990 Trust; barely any money, slightly chaotic, but real and on-point with understanding race equality. It was exciting – oh and by the way, I was still a ticket tout earning about £500 a week just working the weekends. I was leading a double life, and I loved it. I couldn't mix the two, they were worlds apart. I did recruit a few volunteers to go and buy me tickets at *Les Mis* for a tenner or twenty quid, but I had to be careful who I could trust.

* * *

At the end of my first year at Charter 88, something happened that proved a catalyst for a change of direction in my work. On 5 December 1995, a young Black man called Wayne Douglas collapsed and died at Brixton Police Station. He had been arrested on suspicion of burglary, was held down repeatedly, face down, and suffered heart failure (at the inquest, the jury found that his death was caused by police restraint but recorded a verdict of accidental death). Just over a week later, a peaceful picket of the police station turned into a riot, bringing back memories for many of the Brixton riots of 1981 and 1985. The sense of gross injustice at another young Black person dying in a place where he should have be protected from harm cannot be overestimated. It's almost only now, after witnessing the murder of George Floyd in May 2020 that the world can see what police brutality really looks like.

It's not just the death, awful as that is, it is also the dehumanising process that led to the death of Wayne, George and other Black people. Too often, these young men are not seen as fellow human beings, with mothers, fathers, wives and children, but instead they are seen through the prism of a 'thing', or a beast that can be beaten or restrained to within an inch of their lives. And when the default force is so great, knowing exactly where that 'inch of a person's life' is becomes a live-or-die lottery within brutal encounters with law enforcement.

But out of this awful tragedy was born a Black political project that would over time become an institution: Operation Black Vote.

Derek Hinds, who was Lee Jasper's right-hand man at the time, and was there with him on that Brixton night, echoed a Malcolm X refrain, saying we need to use the ballot box and not the bullet. Meaning that rioting in our own neighbourhood, while venting anger, was in effect an act of self-harm. What Hinds sought to propagate was a democratic assault on power. One which targeted the very heart of British power – Parliament – to use our democratic franchise, not to ask for justice but democratically demand it.

So, for the first time in any coordinated, solely race-focused way we began a conversation about how Black people could achieve political power to hold people in authority – the police, politicians, schools, hospitals, jails and more – to account. For all of this, political power was key. At the time, there were just four ethnic minority MPs in Parliament, out of a total of 659 – Diane Abbott, Paul Boateng, Keith Vaz and Bernie Grant.

We couldn't wait for better representation within the establishment, or for our politicians to wake up one morning and decide to seriously address inequality and racism – we had to find another route.

So a meeting was held with people such as Lee Jasper, the activists Derek Hinds and Rita Patel, Dave Weaver, the chat show host Chrystal Rose, and me. Because I was volunteering at Charter 88, it was deemed that I would have greater access to find out just how much political power Black people had. There was a long-held view that Black people were powerless, that our numbers were so small that we could barely make a dent in the electoral process. Our hunch was that might be different, given our numbers were swelling in London, Birmingham and my own town, Leicester. I was keen to impress Lee and all the others too, so I set to work trying to find out just how politically powerful Black, Asian and minority ethnic individuals were within our political system at the time.

I spent over three months on this one project. In the days before the widespread use of the internet, this was a big manual task. I had some luck as there was a great guy who worked in the Houses of Parliament library – I can only remember his first name, Brynn – who had done some research for an MP and was able to forward a lot of information to me about where Black people lived in the country based on the UK census. So, having spent a month struggling to piece together what Brynn had already formulated, all I had to do was get the data showing the majority held by each sitting MP in all the marginal seats and then simply cross-reference the two, with adjustments for voting age. At the end I was able to produce a rough equation, calculating the number of Black, Asian and non-white voters against the marginality of the seat.

I knew it was a eureka moment, a game changer in British politics. I punched the air in sheer delight.

If this was right and we could implement it, i.e. empower

Black communities to demand policies that tackled racial inequalities, we wouldn't have to rely solely on marching or, worse still, rioting to get justice. We could democratically insist upon it. The data clearly showed that if Black people were registered and voted in over seventy seats, it was mathematically plausible the Black vote could in effect decide who won and who lost.

To visualise the potential impact you have to realise that at that time Prime Minister John Major's Conservative Party had won the 1992 general election with a majority of just twenty-one seats. Of the seventy seats I identified, about thirty had been described by the political parties as those that may well decide the next general election.

Never before in British history could anybody say with credible evidence that the Black vote could decide who wins and who loses a general election. And now I had this very evidence sitting in front of me.

And so Lee Jasper and I set up Operation Black Vote, a groundbreaking initiative that would change the course of my life and the face of Britain's political landscape forever. When the Black electorate did vote, it voted overwhelmingly (about 90 per cent) for Labour, but we felt that past Labour governments had not served our communities fantastically well. There was still only four Black and Asian MPs and institutional racism was still shocking in many areas. Our judgement twenty-six years ago was that we wanted all the main-stream political parties to vie for the Black vote, not just Labour. In many ways, Labour had consistently taken the

Black vote for granted – 'If you don't vote for us, who are you going to vote for, the nasty Tory Party?' So back then we began to create a narrative that would entice the Tory Party to believe they could have political capital by appealing to Black voters. I would directly tell every Conservative leader over the next two decades, from John Major to Theresa May, that Black and Asian communities are conservative with a small c by instinct. Law and order, religion, family, education. My rhetorical question to Conservative leaders was: given that, why do you think we don't even consider voting for you? The answer: because we see you as the nasty party, xenophobic by instinct, constantly ignoring talent right in front of your noses. Politically, it was one of the best decisions we made. You just have to look across the Atlantic and see that the Republicans saw no political capital in courting the African-American vote, and so divisions deepen, policies remain deeply tribal, society is failed.

Don't get me wrong, systemic race inequality is not a thing of the past, and in recent years we're going in the wrong direction when it comes to Stop and Search and Black youth unemployment. But having a representation from all the political parties, particularly the main two, is today almost a foregone conclusion.

* * *

We launched Operation Black Vote at the Houses of Commons on 16 July 1996. We wanted to get every political party vying for the Black vote. Our mantra was nothing less than we would decide the next general election. With so many marginal seats in urban areas and a Black population that was condensed in those areas, we had a golden opportunity we just couldn't pass up. It gave us, in a certain sense, almost disproportionate clout. I believed we, as Black British citizens, had to stop rioting and use the power for change right there in front of us.

The name of our new organisation was very deliberate. For many years, the police had termed their activities in Black communities – such as flooding Brixton with police and stopping and searching over 1,000 people in six days, or 'fitting up' countless Black men and women with drugs – 'Operation this' or 'Operation that'. In a conversation about the Metropolitan Police, Derek Hinds said, 'Commissioner Paul Condon has "Operation Eagle Eye" which is criminalising black youth; we need to set up in response a bigger operation – "Operation Black Vote": [Paul Condon] named our organisation.'

Operation Black Vote was a really small entity, just myself, Derek Hinds, Ashok Viswanathan, Rita Patel and Audrey Adams – her son Rolan was killed by racist thugs two years before Stephen Lawrence – on the board behind the scenes, with Lee Jasper as our charismatic figurehead. We had no start-up money, no money on its way, but we were energised and full of ideas. We were determined to unite our communities and make real and lasting change.

In July 1996, there was another talisman that would give us the boost that we were on the right track.

Nelson Mandela visited Brixton's recreation centre as part of his first state visit to the UK. It was an incredible carnival atmosphere, with a crowd of around 10,000 dancing to calypso and reggae. We managed to sneak in and unveil our Operation Black Vote banner. The ticket tout blagging and climbing through windows paid dividends once again. Right in front of me was the greatest living Black person on earth, and there was I, with my banner unfurled and my arm stretched out to shake the great man's hand. Mandela spoke in a quiet voice: 'Go well, my son,' before moving on. Of course we spun that 'Go well' as meaning Nelson Mandela supports Operation Black Vote, along with the picture of my outstretched handshake. What I didn't realise until I was sent a series of pictures from that day was the man behind Mandela was Prince Charles. I'd have to wait some twenty-five years before we met again. But back then on that unforgettable day, I only had eyes for my hero, Nelson Mandela.

The general election was called on 17 March 1997: it would take place on 1 May. We were ready to hit the ground running, targeting those marginal seats where we'd identified that the Black vote could make the difference. We sent out thousands of leaflets to get people to register to vote – it was our first campaign and we had no idea how effective this would be, we just knew we wanted to flood the place with information. We recruited some fantastic volunteers, who literally went door to door, telling people about our meetings and persuading them to register to vote.

I was happy to lead from the front; for me, this was another iteration of 'bob-a-job week' week, or selling showers, coffee machines or theatre tickets. This time, though, I was selling power, hope and a brighter, fairer future – we were unstoppable.

In around ten constituencies we decided to hold public meetings with all the key candidates of the main political parties and invite a Black audience. If any of the candidates didn't come, we would put an empty chair on stage. My gosh, those meetings were so powerful! One of the first big ones was in Croydon town hall with the sitting MP for Croydon North West, Labour's Malcolm Wicks, who was fighting for his seat against the smallest of margins. Malcolm was a lovely guy (sadly, he died in 2012), but boy, did he sweat under the lights of the TV cameras as he was held accountable to Black voters for the first time in such a powerful way.

We drove all around the country to meet with community groups, forge alliances and hold these meetings. Another very memorable one was in Batley and Spen, where we were helped by a young Asian lawyer, Sayeeda Warsi, who was fighting for Asian women's rights. When it came to commanding oratory, Sayeeda was from another planet. In fighting the good fight, she was so impressive. We've now become very dear friends and are nearly always on the same side in debates in the Lords. She is more like a crossbench peer than a tribal Tory peer. A few years ago, when she was Chair of the Conservative Party, she came over to Bethnal

Green – our then HQ – for a seminar meeting. She gave a preamble before the speech: 'I've known Simon for over twenty years. Back then, he used to fancy me like mad,' she said to howls of laughter from the audience. 'Now it seems he's moved on to Naomi Campbell.' More howls of laughter. (I'd invited Naomi Campbell to Downing Street and there had been pictures in the press.) It's a good job you can't see a Black man blush, because I was blushing. I'd never said anything to Sayeeda, I always sought to be professional, but clearly my demeanour gave me away.

Back then, you would never have believed that she would ever be a Conservative politician; she was radical in her demands for social and racial justice. A firebrand who helped us get the buy-in from Asian communities and more generally to make connections in the North of England. Sayeeda taught me that those coming from London, what skin colour or religion they held, were at a disadvantage. They were not trusted. Simple. But you could gain trust by listening, and coming back, time and time again. She was right, of course, and that investment and her connections helped us build an invaluable trust with many communities in the area.

It was around this time that I got a call from two young, dynamic ad creatives, Jon Daniel and Trevor Robinson, who wanted to do our campaign pro bono. Almost from nowhere, we had been talking to one of London's leading agencies, Bartle Bogle Hegarty, who had given us the five-star pro-bono treatment – their best creative team, a production company and what to us seemed like an enormous budget. But as much as we were flattered by their attentions and the money their support would offer, the company felt very white and we were unsure that they would get what we were all about. So when these two energetic, creative Black guys said, 'We can give you a Black product that will empower our people and catapult OBV onto the main political stage,' we believed them. And they didn't disappoint. They did two massive campaigns for us during that election. The premise was to sow the seed that we had power, and leverage, something many had doubted – things were done to us, don't forget, things like police brutality. We were saying that we could show our power, we could be a positive force in society, simply by engaging in politics and voting.

The first was a series of posters that showed the faces of each of the three political leaders with the phone numbers of their constituency office. The simple message was: imagine what it would be like if one million Black people called up Tony Blair, John Major or Paddy Ashdown to tell them what we think. The line at the bottom of the poster read: 'Operation Black Vote: Let them know you exist'. We were told that John Major's constituency office had to get a new phone line because they were bombarded with people calling, saying, 'I want to speak to the Prime Minister.'

Jon and Trevor gave us 'political skin in the democrat game'. I swear, I don't know how they did it but they also made a short film for us. The scene has a prime minister waking up from a nightmare, because he loses the keys to No.10 because he ignored the Black vote.

The political mood was changing. All of a sudden, politicians, more attune to self-preservation, were falling over themselves to be nice to Black people. John Major talked up his Brixton roots; Tony Blair was saying, look at my race credentials I've always been anti-apartheid, and Paddy Ashdown went on College Green and had a picture taken with Black and Asian Liberal Democrat candidates – all of them in unwinnable seats. They were just cannon fodder, but it was all about the optics. Ashdown reasoned that they might not win this time ... but next time never came, as a matter of fact.

Never before in British political history were so many senior politicians and those in marginal seats speaking about Black and Asians communities in the positive. They could see the potential benefit. In past elections, and future ones too, Brexit in particular, adopting an anti-foreigner stance was an electoral winner. That tide was turning, albeit, if I'm honest, at times in a rather superficial way. There were slogans like 'Black and Asian communities make a wonderful contribution to our society. Vote Labour, Tory or Lib Dems'. But it was a start.

* * *

That campaign launched Operation Black Vote and it was making a big noise all over the place. I was now a political activist, learning the ropes and campaigning hard for something I believed in. And yet to make that happen, I was living a double life. To pay the bills, I was still working at night as a West End ticket tout. It was essential, as it not only gave me the platform to be political because I didn't have to worry about money, but being part of this world gave me the confidence to do what I needed to during the day, dealing with all these powerful people. You see, being a successful ticket tout you had to have swagger – the punters were not just buying a ticket, often at four times the face value, they were buying your trust that this was the best deal on the street.

For the most part, I never let my two, very different, worlds overlap. On a couple of occasions, I told some of my colleagues at Charter 88 when we were in the pub after work having a drink that I sold tickets outside *Les Misérables*. I remember one conversation in particular about my 'second job' with an all-white group. One of the women almost started to cry. 'Wow, Simon! How can you do that?' she said. 'You're such a decent guy. How do you reconcile that? You're a tout. You're a spiv … in the West End?'

It was almost as though they couldn't see that anybody in that world, hustling on the streets of the West End, ducking and diving, could be a decent human being. In truth, my experience was that generosity in both spirit and material things – buying drinks, lending money – was found more often than not among my working-class friends rather than within this middle-class polite world that I was now gravitating in.

At the same time, the guys I knew from working outside

the theatres of central London couldn't reconcile that I'd been studying for a degree and had now gone into political activism. It was a weird time for me because I lived in both realities; one made the other possible and both made me who I am today.

I look back fondly on the relationships I had in the West End. There was one particular South Londoner called Alfie Kelly, who was mixed heritage. I'm not sure where his father was from but his mother was Irish. He was the fastest-talking, sharpest guy I ever met and watching him assess people and judge situations was a masterclass in understanding human behaviour. And yet in other ways he was like many of us: flawed. Sometimes we would finish the day with lots of money and I needed little encouragement to go out drinking with him. If I ever decided to go, I knew I'd have to write off a couple of days because we would go from one club to another, to the crazy places; glamorous clubs, but also those that were either seedy or gangster-filled. Everybody knew Alfie and loved him. When we went to the more dodgy places, the door person would say to him: 'Who's your mate?' Alfie would reply, 'He's cool, he's with me.' I remember once trying to go back to one place without Alfie and they simply said, said no!

I loved dipping into this world but I knew it wasn't the full-time lifestyle I'd choose.

Those outside their world were called 'Straight goer', people who kept to all the rules, but in reality, most struggled to make ends meet. I guess I was lucky to gravitate in both these very different worlds; the smart move was to cherry pick the best of both.

* * *

Election day was fast approaching and the political parties were trying to squeeze everything they could to get any political advantage. And the Black vote was counting. A few weeks before the election, I got a call from the Shadow Home Secretary's office: Jack Straw wanted to speak to me, Simon – nobody – Woolley. I held the phone up in the air in some disbelief: 'Jack Straw's on the phone' I mimed to the team. A very polite and matter-of-fact Shadow Home Secretary stated, 'Mr Woolley, we've been very impressed with your efforts to get minority ethnic communities to register to vote and come out and vote.' *I'm sure you are,* I thought. *If they do vote, you know that they are much more likely to vote for you.* With these thoughts I let him finish. 'Simon,' he said, 'I'd like you to hold a press conference for an announcement I'd like to make.'

'What might that be, Mr Straw?' I enquired.

Simply put, he said, 'If Black people vote Labour, I will promise to deliver a public inquiry into the death of Stephen Lawrence.'

Credit to Jack Straw, he delivered on his promise, which became transformative change. Even in my wildest dreams OBV could not take the credit for that – I have said we played our part. In truth, the credit for this goes to Lord Paul Boateng, Bernie Grant and Baroness Lawrence …

and finally, the great man Nelson Mandela, who during his visit gave it the prominence that it lacked at the time. Their lobbying convinced Jack Straw to help deliver seismic change in British society – we were just a platform to speak to Black voters.

And then came election night, 1 May 1997. We had thrown absolutely everything we had at mobilising the Black vote and making sure politicians knew they had to listen to communities they had previously ignored. With hardly any money and relying heavily on a team of volunteers working for free, we had distributed something like 250,000 voter registration cards, 500,000 leaflets and 50,000 posters. We'd had around 200 articles written about the work of OBV in the national and international press and done what felt like countless radio and TV interviews.

We hired a bar in Brixton – I say we hired, that's not entirely true. We were given the bar with TVs so we could watch the election night coverage. The bar was rammed, which was unprecedented for a political party night in the 1990s. The night was unbelievably exciting. The vast majority wanted Labour to win. For many, the Tories were the nasty party: Blair offered hope.

As the night unfolded, it became clear that not only were Labour going to win a more significant victory than most pundits had predicted, but some big political beasts were going to fall. Six Cabinet ministers lost their seats, but the biggest shock of the night was, famously, when Cabinet Minister Michael Portillo lost in Enfield Southgate. These days, Portillo is like the cuddly uncle, with his pink trousers, but back then, he'd voted against gay rights even though he later admitted he'd had an affair with a guy himself. (He was beaten that night by Labour's Stephen Twigg, who is 'openly' gay – as they used to say in those days.) There was a pandemonium of joy that the 'nasty people' from the 'nasty party' – as Theresa May would later infamously call it – those who seemed not to care about social and racial injustice, would be leaving government.

The Labour Party had hired Royal Festival Hall so when the bar in Brixton had to close, we all went down there. It must have been about four or five in the morning as it was starting to get light and hundreds if not thousands of people swelled and swirled around Festival Hall. I was probably a little bit worse for wear for drinking until 5am but I gave an interview to the BBC, saying that the Black vote made a difference. It was a euphoric moment, completely out of this world.

In the cold light of reality, it was clear that Tony Blair had won with a landslide – a 179-seat majority, the largest held by any government for over sixty years. This was great news as it marked the start of what felt like a progressive new era. The new Home Secretary, Jack Straw, kept his promise for a public inquiry into the death of Stephen Lawrence, which felt like a hugely important step forward. It was the first time in British history that Black politics had come to the fore and we were very proud of everything Operation Black Vote had achieved. And yet, we felt a little deflated. While we'd got hundreds of thousands to register to vote and put Black politics on the map, the huge swing to Labour meant we couldn't point to the big impact we'd had in the way we had envisaged we would be able to.

Looking back now, I can see that, in some ways, this may have been one of the most important moments for Operation Black Vote. Had we claimed victory as we had hoped, this might have led us to focus almost exclusively on elections every four years. We would have thought, that's what you do; that's how you gain power. But because things worked out differently, we began to think differently. We looked beyond the election cycle and developed a vision that was so much bigger than that.

We understood that to truly tackle racial injustice, we needed a campaign that would look at three fundamentals to empower a society, and so the pillars of Operation Black Vote were born: political participation, political education and political representation. These three pillars still drive the organisation today. Participation meant, of course, continuing our efforts with voter registration and turnout for every election – local and national. If we could go into schools and colleges, we could help people who often felt disenfranchised and let down by our political system better understand how power works, where it lies and how we can unlock it to bring about the change we need to see.

It had not really dawned on me until I worked with Charter 88 that in Britain we were subjects to the Crown.

With no constitution and no Bill of Rights, our rights as citizens had to be protected, and unless people understand where the power lies, it's very difficult to take it. To put it bluntly, my beloved UK – particularly among Black, Asian and minority ethnic communities, but also among many within the working class – was politically illiterate. That's not to blame us, the system was set up that way, bolstered by twenty years or more of hundreds of negative headlines, both in the tabloids but also in broadsheets that blamed the least empowered for all of society's ills. Worse still, those most negatively affected by policies emanating from high above are often the least likely to vote. I'm tired of hearing the erroneous mantra of 'If voting made a difference, they'd ban it'.

To this day I'm shockingly disappointed that citizenship education is not a central tenant to our children's education from primary school, and will campaign for it with my dying breath.

The final pillar to our foundation was the mantra that anywhere there are decisions being made that affect our lives, we should be at the table. We saw that it wasn't just in Westminster where our communities needed representing, it was at local authority level and particularly in the courts. We felt we knew a lot about racial injustice when it came to law and the courts so why were we never the ones dispensing it? Operation Black Vote was still an organisation largely driven by the passion and commitment of volunteers with no money to speak of, so to set out a fifteen- to twenty-year strategy as we did then was audacious, to say the least, but we knew what we wanted to achieve and we believed we knew how to do it. Again, it was another brainwave from Derek Hinds, who constantly reminded me how the Japanese government become a global powerhouse after the Second World War simply by having a twenty-year strategy: 'If they could do it,' Hinds said, 'so could we.'

With this in place, one of our first steps was selling this story to No.10. One of our key routes into Downing Street was through Faz Hakim, who had been a political advisor to the chair and chief executive at the Equality and Human Rights Commission and served as director of corporate and government relations at the Commission for Racial Equality, then went on to become one of Blair's special advisors (SpAds). We had long conversations and as a result of our lobbying, and her trust in me, in September 1997, at the first Labour Party conference since the Party took office, we had what felt like a breakthrough. In Tony Blair's keynote speech, setting out his store for the next four years of government, he talked about how Britain must be a beacon to the rest of the world, but said: 'We cannot be a beacon to the world unless the talents of all the people shine through. Not one Black High Court Judge; not one Black Chief Constable or Permanent Secretary. Not one Black Army officer above the rank of Colonel. Not one Asian either. Not a record of pride for the British establishment. And not a record of pride for the British Parliament that there are so few black and Asian MPs.' No prime minister had ever been so bold on race equality before. Hakim contacted me afterwards and said: 'You happy now, Simon? Now you've got to help us deliver on this ambitious agenda.'

Operation Black Vote was barely a year old at this point. We were far from being astute operators with access to the big players, knowing how to pull the levers in the machine to get what we wanted. No one was being paid and all we really knew was how to make a noise. We had a lot to learn when it came to translating our aims into direct action that would have real impact on the institutions in which we wanted to see change, but we'd done enough for a national reset of sorts and we had our aims in place.

After 1997, I started trying to go to Labour Party conferences as much as I could. I was the tiniest of fish in the biggest pond, but had learned enough to know that, whenever you could, you had to go to where the power is. One year I was in Brighton or Manchester and saw the Lord Chancellor, Lord Irvine, who had been a friend of Tony Blair since the early 1980s when Blair was Irvine's pupil at 11 King's Bench Walk Chambers. He was walking away from me down a corridor so I thought I'd better run after him, otherwise he'd be gone and I'd miss a great opportunity. So I literally chased him down.

His mandarins all around him had a look of great alarm when they saw this Black guy coming towards him, even though I was in my normal smart attire, which for many of us is a Black thing – we like dressing sharp, and we also know that we don't have the luxury of looking Dominic

Cummings' 'Scruffy chic' if we want to be taken seriously
– although a fat lot of good my sharp attire was helping
in that precise moment. Truth is, I'm pretty sure if there
was a police panic button it would have been pressed,
with officers running to the scene, tasers drawn. I had to
calm down the situation and quick: humour. With hands
in the air, showing I meant no harm, I said: 'Guys, guys,
calm down, take a cigarette break. It's all good. My name's
Simon Woolley. I run Operation Black Vote and I have a
great idea for you, Lord Chancellor, that will transform the
magistracy by getting many more Black, Asian and minority
ethnic magistrates into the courts.' Everyone around took a
collective sigh of relief. Lord Irvine looked me up and down
and simply said, 'Well, what's not to like about that? What's
your name?'

'Simon Woolley, sir, Operation Black Vote.'

'Well, Simon Woolley, Operation Black boat,' he
mistakenly replied, 'If you can pull that off, you'll get my
support.' He turned to his special advisor, 'Get Simon's
details and meet with him in London.' And with that, the
less than three-minute corridor pitch that very nearly never
began, the deal was done.

His team loved the idea, and word got back to us that
Lord Irvine thought I was a brilliant chancer. I'll take that
all day long, I thought.

With funding from the Ministry of Justice we started
a five-year campaign to get magistrates from Black, Asian
and minority ethnic communities onto the bench. Oh, and

finally, we were getting paid. More often than not we took people who had no idea that they could be a magistrate, much less know what the process was. But my pitch to them was compelling: We painfully knew what injustice looked like when many young Black people went to the courts and were fitted up by the police and given greater sentences than their white peers. We said we must not only start dispensing justice, but at the same time help transform the thinking within the courts with better understanding from people's own lived experience.

The process was fairly straightforward. With the help of the Magistrates Association, who I have to say were terrific, we trained them in what went on in the courts. Then working with the local courts, we twinned them with a sitting magistrate – we called it 'shadowing'. And then crucially, we helped them with their applications and interviews. You have to remember, our cohorts knew nothing about this world, its language or procedures. Our objective was to look for individuals who had a great sense of civic duty and a good heart to deliver, strong but fair justice in courts up and down the land.

Over that five-year period, from a starting point of zero, over 150 magistrates became Justices of the Peace. Many of them are now heads of the courts, transforming the perception of what a magistrate – a judge – 'looks like' and bringing their own knowledge and experience into places that were previously virtually all white.

One of the second cohort of women to be selected,

Sharon Wallace, tells a wonderful story which captures the reality at that time. It's a story I've retold at least a hundred times. On her first day as a Justice of the Peace, she was in a court anteroom with her colleagues and she received a tap on the shoulder from a white official, who said to her very politely, 'Excuse me, members of the public shouldn't be in here. Please can you move outside?'

Sharon said, 'I'm not a member of the public,' and flashed her ID badge to show she was allowed into the room, though it didn't identify her as a magistrate.

Twenty or so minutes later and it was time to go into court. The protocol is that magistrates have to go through their door at the back to enter the well before they sit on the benches. When she emerged in front of the assembled court, she saw the woman who had informed her she did not belong in the official space, and watched her jaw drop as she realised that not only was Sharon absolutely entitled to belong, but she was in fact one of Her Majesty's Justices of the Peace – a magistrate. Sharon stared impassively in front, with the quiet dignity of someone who was about to do her civic duty. But behind that impassive look, somewhere deep inside Sharon's soul, was a bursting joy that said: 'Yes, Yes! Attitudes will have to change.'

There's a wonderful footnote to Sharon's story/journey. About three years ago she became Chair of the Bristol Magistrates court, and began work with another Operation Black Vote alumni, Mayor Marvin Rees, and his Deputy, Asher Craig. Together, they began the most successful

BAME local recruitment, particularly for African and Caribbean magistrates, ever. The ethos of blazing trails, but also ensuring that others follow, is wonderfully ensconced in the City of Bristol.

For us at Operation Black Vote these were very special days. And above all, watching young men and women from our communities literally grow in front of your eyes is a gift from heaven.

It is right that I give a very special mention to three extraordinary women who helped not just the magistrates' shadowing scheme but the kaleidoscope of leadership schemes that OBV has run. They are Winsome-Grace Cornish, Francine Fernandes and Merlene Carrington – the latter two started out as participants on OBV's scheme. Merlene, who served for a decade as a magistrate, is still with OBV today, twenty years later.

For many years, well after the scheme stopped due to funding, we would get calls from individuals who'd been part of it, saying, 'Simon, I don't know whether this is of major interest, but because of you, because of Operation Black Vote, yesterday I was sworn in as one of Her Majesty's Justices of the Peace ...' Every time I heard that I'd think, *wow, that's special, really very special.*

* * *

The leadership schemes we would develop over a twenty-year period all came from that twenty-year strategy we thought about and devised after Blair's landslide election victory using our three pillars: Political Participation – voter registration; Political Representation – leadership schemes; and Political Education – citizenship in schools.

Our north star for political representation was of course not magistrates, important as they were, it was MPs. Remember, when we started in 1996, there were only four. So our first leadership scheme was an MP shadowing scheme. The scheme was designed with two clear objectives: first, nurture the next generation of BAME political representatives for both local and national government; second, but equally important, showcase and lobby the political parties that there was a deluge of Black talent right in front of their noses, and if they wanted the Black vote, they should create their own pathways for this talent to serve as parliamentarians. Today, there are sixty-five Black, Asian and minority ethnic MPs, the largest in any Western European country by a long stretch. Ten per cent of those MPs come directly from OBV schemes. Others have gone on to leading positions outside of Parliament, such as former Haringey leader Joe Ejiofor, and present Bristol Mayor, and I think future leader of the Labour Party and therefore potential Prime Minister, Marvin Rees.

I met the young Rees twenty years ago when he came knocking at my door, stating he wanted change, and could I help. 'Could I help?' I said. 'Young man, I'm going to ensure it happens.'

The working-class son of an English mother and Jamaican

father, Rees made history as the first directly elected mayor of a European city of Caribbean or African heritage. A city that many more people have a greater awareness of its extremely dark history as a result of Black Lives Matter protestors pulling down the statue of the enslaver-turned-Bristol-philanthropist, Edward Colston.

It's interesting for me looking at those pictures of a fresh-faced enthusiastic Rees engaging with the Prime Minister of the day, Tony Blair, knowing that it could be his destiny too. But it nearly all went very pear-shaped with Marvin, even before it really started. He had finished on the MP Shadowing scheme, he also signed up for anything else that we were doing or he'd just show up: 'Heard you had a meeting with Black Church leaders, you don't mind if I tag along, do you?' How can you possibly say no, right?

Anyway, one evening, I get a call from Marvin, and he's about excited as excitement can be – in the manner of a teenager coming home to tell their parents they are predicted to get three A stars or something like that.

'Simon, Simon, I've got some great news! I just thought you'd want to know. I mean, wow, I didn't expect it so soon, but hey, seizing opportunities right, Simon? As you've always said …'

I interrupted his breathless flow with a 'So, what is it?'

'I've been selected to fight the very winnable council seat in the local elections.'

'Marvin, this is great news, history in the making. You

know you'll be the first Black male councillor and then they'll be two of you.'

To which he now interjected with an 'Ahh, that's where there's a slight problem. The Labour Party would like me to fight against the only Black councillor out of seventy representatives and they are sure I can win. I know it's not ideal, Simon, but what do you honestly think?'

And for the first and last time, with Marvin at least, I said nothing. My heart sank, and my blood began to boil. *Those bastards*, I thought. *This brilliant young man, his own political team are brutally reminding him, one: who's in charge?, and two: race equality really doesn't matter. One in, one out, all good for the status quo.*

Psychologically, of course, this was another 'how would you like to pay, cash or terms?' moment. Whoever spoke first would lose. Except, not quite this time. I held my nerve with the deafening silence between two friends, mentor and mentee.

In the end Marvin broke the silence, with an 'OK, OK. I know. It's beyond being wrong what they're offering, and I really knew it was. I just wanted your view, Simon. That's all. Thanks a million, as always.' And with that, he put the phone down.

What Marvin did next would both haunt him and me, but at the very same time empower him to be, in part, the brilliant young leader he is today.

He called the Labour Party and said, 'With all my heart and soul I will fight any seat you give me, except against the only other Black councillor.' They never gave him another seat to fight, and he was in effect ostracised from the Party for a number of years, even barring him from standing for a parliamentary seat.

When he was barred from standing because of 'disloyalty' to the Party, I did question whether I'd used my privilege to silently demand Marvin confront his own integrity was the right thing to do – after all, I wasn't going to be affected by the obvious consequences. But the thought of my actions contributing to holding back this powerhouse of brilliance was quite a bit to deal with.

Of course, it worked out really well in the end.

What's interesting though when on the day of the announcement of whether or not Marvin had won, bearing in mind four years earlier he'd lost the same Mayoral race, he called me up as the count was being finalised. He said that the count was going well, but it was not 100 per cent. It had been twenty years since we first started this journey together, and in his moment of glory, Marvin called to say, 'Simon, we've done it. We've won. Now let's go and do the work.' Marvin is not my son, we're not even related, beyond the 'black brotherhood', but I felt as proud as any dad would be of his son just getting elected to high office. I knew he had the skill, and the ambition, but his often rollercoaster journey ensured his integrity was both intact and strengthened.

Looking back now, I can only conclude that we were ambitious beyond belief and/or slightly deluded that a team of six individuals, half of whom were part-time, could dramatically move the political, cultural and even educational dial with our ideas and action plans.

Viewed through the most critical lens, some have said too many people in the UK are politically illiterate; in most elections around 40 per cent of those registered don't vote. That rate rises to 70 per cent in local elections, and voting for Police and Crime Commissioners is even worse at 80 per cent not voting. Those figures are significantly worse for many Black, Asian and minority ethnic communities. But it's not just voting where there is a lack of progress, crucial decisions are made in so many areas and not just in democratic institutions, but also within the vast array of public bodies making decisions about, well, almost everything under our sun.

So we began an audacious plan, primarily targeting youths; young Black and white students in any school in the count, to better understand power: how it works, where it lies, how we, as ordinary citizens, can access and influence it.

Our view has been we need to start with students to better understand the political and civic landscape they will inherit, and hopefully run it much better than we've seen. Our idea then was to produce a booklet, an interactive booklet that did what it says on the tin – 'Understanding Power' – aimed particularly at schools and colleges. Straightforward and digestible, it would help young people understand power through a prism they were comfortable with: music, fashion, the police, culture. Looking back at it now, it's still a pretty good document and stands the test of time. As we talked through and put together the document it also helped us learn and take a bird's eye view of what we understood as power. I think it massively helped that we had two young guys driving the project.

One of these was Faz Hakim, whose sister, also curiously named Faz Hakim, was one of Blair's SpAds. We got a couple of the members from the grime band So Solid Crew to help us promote it and went around the country with this document. We produced about 50,000 copies that went into 500 schools to really ignite the idea of citizenship from a young person's point of view. My friend, the late Jon Daniel, who devised our advertising campaign back in 1996–97, did the design for this too and made a brilliant video. We wanted young people to better understand our political institutions and get the message out that, as citizens, we are the democratic masters and the politicians are 'the servants flicking the switch', as Jon Daniel put it.

* * *

In the first three or four years of Operation Black Vote, things moved very fast. We were either volunteers working at Charter 88 – Ashok Viswanathan and myself – or those such as Derek Hinds and Joe Ejiofor working on the 1990 Trust. None of us were puffed up for example, I didn't call myself the 'director' then as I didn't feel I had the credibility or the prestige for such a title, so I called myself the coordinator, along with Lee Jasper.

Andrew Puddephatt, the Left-leaning leader of Charter 88, was well respected in the democratic world, a good thinker and a good man, and he lent his support, and I should add his wisdom, to Operation Black Vote in those early days. Jenny Watson who was also at Charter 88 was probably our biggest supporter there. But Charter 88 remained a white organisation, technically non-partisan but practically left of centre. It felt towards the end that we were tolerated there rather than really embraced. I don't think they ever raised any funds for us and their middle-class thinking seemed to be that race inequality needed to be dealt with but not by them, or even by a project within them. The ethos around it's everyone's role to ensure Black Lives Matter came too late for Charter 88, but when talking about this, the simple truth remains I'm pretty sure we could not have launched OBV without the support and energy of Charter 88. It's just I was frustrated that the democratic demands and reform that were central to Charter 88, giving voice to the voiceless, were also central to tackling systemic racism.

During Prime Minister Tony Blair's ambition programme for devolved power the first mayoral election had just begun. And after failing to become Labour's candidate for the 2000 London mayoral election, Ken Livingstone stood as an independent – and won. He took Lee Jasper and his wonderful 'every day there's a new fight' energy with him to City Hall, leaving me, Derek and Karen Chouhan, who was then head of the 1990 Trust, to continue our work building Operation Black Vote.

Lee Jasper is a larger-than-life figure and when it comes to front line race equality activism he is peerless. In regard to OBV, he was the driving force in the inception and I guess was a key foot soldier. I looked up to him as a hero and a mentor, but while our relationship has always been full of mutual respect, it has also been at times quite challenging.

On a weekly basis, Lee would call or come into the office: 'Right guys, we're doing this. A family needs us in Nottingham, so we're going up there to hold a public meeting. Simon, you do this; Karen, this is your role.' It was fantastically empowering. We'd set the event, get local politicians and media, and Lee would speak, raising the roof, pointing the finger at individuals or institutions – normally the police – who needed to be called out. But at times it was scattergun, and not easy to build projects as some of us would have liked.

When he went to City Hall, he took his wonderful but often chaotic energy with him. And I guess following Lee's departure, I was forced to find my own voice and place in this arena of race equality. I was able to come out of the shadows and develop who I was, and my own vision. But I still had a lot to learn, not least about how to lead an organisation that had grown very organically from people who were never paid and who wanted to do big things. There was never an internal strategy as there would be in business, or if you were setting up a new institution from scratch. In those early days, I thought everyone had the same energy and 'we're not stopping until the job's done well' attitude. I expected everyone to be there first thing in the morning – I'm an early riser – and ready to hit the ground running. It's the way I operate and I would be disappointed if I didn't see someone go the extra mile – well, extra ten miles, really – completing a task in the same way I would do it myself. But fortunately I was surrounded by amazing people who taught me a lot about being a good director.

One of them was Ashok Viswanathan, who I mentioned before. He'd joined Charter 88 before I did, as a young rebel student working on the youth wing. After completing his degree, he joined the National Association against Racism, but for most of his adult life he has worked for Operation Black Vote. He loves what he does and knows where his strengths are. He said to me, 'Simon, not everybody's like you – thank heavens – so stop trying to make others be like you. It's wrong and it's frustrating.' It was what I needed to hear; I thought about what he meant with the sort of self-reflection that hopefully makes you a better person. I then sought to focus on what each individual was good at and nurture that, and to recognise that different people work in different ways.

I've always sought to encourage rather than 'it's my way or the highway'. But I've also realised that some people are going to see my softly-softly approach as a weakness and try and take liberties; thankfully, most people we chose to work around us saw exactly what we were doing and as a result, we cultivated a small but dynamic team with members being with us for many years delivering on an extraordinary level. That includes our board members.

Board members Rita Patel, Audrey Adams, David Weaver and Meena Dhobi have been there from the beginning. They are all incredible, but beyond the board, the day-to-day staff have always done the heavy lifting. Rafiq Maricar started as a volunteer like all of us and he's been with OBV for nearly twenty years. Rafiq is an IT and data guy rather than an activist in the strictest sense, but he's a key part of the team who has also helped me better understand the issues of Muslim communities, both at home and abroad.

We co-opted Winsome-Grace Cornish, who started off as a volunteer even when she left *The Voice* at its zenith, when they were getting hundreds of thousands of readers a week. She stayed for fifteen years until she properly retired. Francine Fernandes joined one of our first MP shadowing schemes and went on to become Operation Black Vote's deputy director. Her talent was quickly spotted and for many years she headed up all Operation Black Vote's leadership programmes; she has personally nurtured many hundreds of graduates from the MP, magistrates and civic leadership shadowing schemes. As CEO, I am often afforded the credit for Operation Black Vote's success, but as I'm sure countless individuals will agree, it was Francine who was central to the success of hundreds of people right across the country. Merlene Carrington was on one of our first magistrates' shadowing schemes. She became a magistrate for a while and then came to work for us, because she knew she wanted to help us to deliver more schemes. Operation Black Vote soon became more professional and more structured, thanks to Francine Fernandes, Winsome Grace-Cornish and Merlene Carrington.

Then there are the hundreds of volunteers that have played their part. We try and give our volunteers an experience that will be life-changing, throwing them in at the deep end, getting them to write, getting them to organise, getting them to speak to celebrities and politicians.

People used to come and visit our offices in Bethnal Green and our little team of eight, and sometimes you could see on their faces a certain disappointment – *this is all Operation Black Vote is? Yet we see you out there and imagine a monster organisation?* There are organisations with thirty, forty, fifty staff that do not have the impact or the visibility Operation Black Vote does, which is testimony to such a wonderfully dedicated team whose core members have all been there for ten, fifteen, twenty years and more. While I have had the good fortune to head this organisation there's a team of people who rightly demand great applause because in many ways they've carried the organisation and they've given me the platform for me to be who I am now.

One of the beauties about being the CEO of an organisation like Operation Black Vote, and the way we organically started life, has always been that anything's possible; that if we can conceive it, we can do it. That blank space, particularly for someone like myself, has been a dream come true.

CHAPTER 6

AMERICA AND ME

In 1998, the Greater London Authority referendum was held to ask the city's residents whether they were in favour of Greater London Authority headed by an elected Mayor of London. At Operation Black Vote, we saw that as a fantastic opportunity for the city, particularly with the knowledge that, as we put it at the time, 'One third of Londoners are Black' or at least non-white, the Black vote would be absolutely crucial when it came to voting in the first London mayor. A Greater London Authority, it was eventually decided, would have oversight of London's police and fire services, a veto on major planning applications, control over various areas of traffic and transport and some management of economic development projects – powers that were currently held by central government, and a general leadership platform. We thought if we can show success in the capital, other cities will see their own political potential.

When the election did finally come we would once again call upon OBV's unsung hero Jon Daniel to put together a stellar advertising campaign with big names giving their services, such as the then global superstar Des'ree, fashion icon Ozwald Boateng and actress, writer and comedienne Meera Syal – the latter did a shoot at Leytonstone underground station, which she remembered fondly as a child.

In the run-up to the referendum our goal was to be a central part of the debate and so we, as ever, dived into the research about other city mayors, particularly those with Black communities. The US readily sprang to our attention when looking for a comparative model: a nation like ours wrestling with deep-seated race inequality; a Black community demanding both representation and policies that would work for them not against them.

Imagine for a second a team of virtual volunteers calling up big cities in the US, asking to speak to and then inviting their leaders to come to London and campaign for Black empowerment. It wasn't as though there was a great reference point for OBV. We'd barely started, we were still squatting at the Charter 88 offices, but it didn't matter one jot. At this time I'd recruited Joe Ejiofor, who would go on to become Haringey's Leader, and Lester Holloway, who has become editor of *The Voice* newspaper. We bashed away to try and get any interest. And finally, we got lucky.

The relatively unknown mayor of Kansas City, Missouri, Emanuel Cleaver, to my amazement agreed to take a trip over to London. As usual, we were operating our campaigns on a shoestring but he was happy to fly economy and he was content with a three-star modest hotel. Years later, he reminds me of that. He is now one of the godfathers of US Black American politics, becoming a Congressman and former head of the Congressional Black Caucus and many other high-level committees. He'll say, 'Brother Simon, boy, you put me to work in London,' and, pointing a finger at me with a broad smile, he'll state, 'You put me up in a hotel that I can only describe as "interesting".'

I picked up Emanuel from the airport and we started campaigning almost straight away, despite the fact he'd just got off a ten-hour flight. We took him to lots of debates with potential mayoral candidates and he was brilliant. He said that Kansas City was not much different to London in its racial makeup and so he recognised that if you got the non-white vote out you could make a difference and begin to bring about more equal representation. He explained that when he had won his election, his city had never had an African-American mayor before and City Hall was very white. He told his team that he wanted his administration to look like the people it sought to serve and that it had to be more diverse, particularly at the top – 'If you don't make it happen, you're out of a job. It's as simple as that.' It worked – within a year, City Hall had begun to look like the citizens it served.

In truth, we knew that Americans are a little bit more direct than us polite Brits, but it showed what you could do with political power, will and vision. I asked him how he responded to any criticisms that he was putting people in certain positions just because they were Black and he explained that the prerequisite for anyone coming through the door was talent. That had to be the starting point. He said that he was making the case not just for diversity but for equality.

As a young activist, listening to Cleaver sing about Black empowerment for both our institutions and best of all our communities was utterly magical. We've been friends ever since.

His visit was significant and inspiring for a number of reasons. It showed us that we could look for help beyond the UK in our fight for race equality within it and it represented the first of several transatlantic relationships that would be hugely valuable, not just for Operation Black Vote as an organisation, but for me personally as I learned and developed as an activist and a leader. Another of those very fruitful relationships that was kicked off with Emanuel's visit was with the American Embassy. We told the Embassy that we were bringing over an African-American mayor and asked if we could have a reception there. They were thrilled and rolled out the red carpet for him, and he gave a wonderful speech.

* * *

Bringing the UK, particularly the Black UK, to the American Embassy seemed to them to be a wonderful opportunity; I'm guessing the Embassy had never had so many Black people inside their then Central London location ever. But with people such as Anthea Buckeridge, head of the International Visitor programme, and Sue Wedlake, then cultural attaché, we were made very welcome.

The American government has a scheme known as the International Visitor Leadership Program (IVLP). It's a professional exchange programme whereby up-and-coming politicians, activists and business people are invited to spend three weeks in the US, starting in Washington, D.C. and then travelling around to different parts of the country to meet people relevant to their line of work for the purpose of creating relationships, potentially with future leaders and getting a flavour of the political systems there. In 2001, I was accepted onto the programme. They gave me two options: go with a group and travel the US, or go by myself and make my own journey up. No brainer! Solo. Make up my own US journey.

I was due to fly to Washington, D.C. on 15 September 2001, four days before the world dramatically, tragically, changed forever.

On 11 September I was with the now Secretary of State for Education, Nadhim Zahawi. We'd become friends since the London Mayoral Campaign, where he and Stephan Shakespeare were big campaigners for Jeffrey Archer. After that, they both set up YouGov, the extremely successful polling company. I was in his office, probably asking for money, which I never got, but in his foyer the pictures of that terrible day were emerging. The early reports were indicating that a light aircraft had accidentally flown into one of the Twin Towers. That faint hope didn't last long.

The sheer scale of the horror of this monumental attack on the US is hard to describe to anyone who is too young to remember it.

Literally a day later or two later, I can't actually remember, I got a call from the American Embassy. Bearing in mind now, all flights, I think around the world had stopped, particularly to and from the US, Sue Wedlake, who had organised my US trip, called to ask, did I still want to go? Nobody would be offended if I said no, by the way. Their reasoning, astonishing as it was, was to say yes and show that America was still open for business, that it would not be cowed by these dreadful terrorist attacks. I said I would go, and four or five days later, I was on one of the first flights to the US after 9/11. I swear to God, you should have seen the way everyone looked at each other on the flight, as if this would be our last journey – it's not a good look.

There was also the gut-sinking feeling of what occurred as we flew into Washington, D.C., past the Pentagon; the gaping gap within it and the dust from the rubble gave the impression it was still smouldering.

It was the most extraordinary time to be in the US. First and foremost, it is probably the only time in America's recent history that you saw this giant of a nation raw, vulnerable and yet impressively united. As a Black Brit arriving in America on a programme designed to foster friendship and international solidarity, I was treated like royalty wherever I went. The effect that trip had on me personally was profound. For one, I came out of my shell as an orator. There were so many occasions when I was asked to speak, and I was privileged to hear some very powerful and moving speeches too. In that situation, at that time of a great nation's vulnerability, it was impossible to do anything but speak instinctively and honestly. Above all else, it felt vital to connect and show solidarity on the most human level. And an experience like that teaches you a lot.

In San Francisco, at the world-famous GLIDE Memorial Church, the Reverend Fitch gave the most compelling speech about how this is a time when we're no longer hyphen Americans, just Americans. As an international guest I was invited to speak, and I focused my remarks on the solidarity we had with the US. I said that during the First and Second World Wars you were there for us, now we are here for you. After I spoke, people came up to me and hugged me, telling me how moved they were by my words.

I went to Atlanta, Georgia, home of Martin Luther King, and made some really good friends there, along with seeing a side of America that you don't see on TV. The US doesn't have a social system as we do that houses and feeds people, and so every day, churches in Atlanta feed their poor. That is their social safety net, the Church.

I criss-crossed the US and drove great lengths, at one

time in a Jaguar – I felt like a king. I flew down to Texas, where my Spanish instantly got me closer to the Hispanic community there, particularly in the schools I visited. But I wasn't always made welcome with open arms. My first time in El Paso – bear in mind this is before anyone had dreamt of dramatising *Narcos: Mexico* on Netflix – I strayed off the beaten track and found myself in what can only be described as a local bar with interesting characters. As I walked in, everyone turned around – I must have looked like a rookie Federal agent. A woman rushed to the kitchen and a big set guy came out to ask, 'Gringo, how can I help you?' I replied, with a naïve smile, '*No estoy Gringo, soy Ingles, Como estas?*' To which he repeated, 'Gringo, how can I help you?' I know what you're thinking. Awkward, right? Right. But I can't just run out, I don't know what would happen. So I sheepishly asked for a 'Beer, please' in my best English accent. I drank that beer as fast and as slow as I could so as not to appear too jittery and then raced back to the hotel. When I told the hotel barman where I'd been he said, 'Are you crazy?'

In other cities I was warmly welcomed ... with one caveat. In the South don't think you can have an open discussion about gun law – you can't. On a more positive note, I made great contacts with the NAACP – the National Association for the Advancement of Colored People. I met with the activist Charles Evers, the older brother of Medgar Evers, another activist, who was murdered in 1963 by the KKK. I also went to meet with people at Morehouse and

Spelman Colleges, the two historic Black colleges in Atlanta. It was a remarkable trip in so many ways and cemented my connection with America.

The following year, I was asked to speak at the State of the Black World Conference in Atlanta, an annual event that's a 'Who's Who' of African-Americans. Reverend Jesse Jackson, Reverend Al Sharpton, Martin Luther King III and California's Democratic congresswoman, Maxine Waters – who, at eighty-three years old, is still a firebrand – were just some of the big names on the conference line-up. There, I faced an audience of about three or four thousand, after Jackson, Sharpton, King and Waters had taken to the dais. It could have been terrifying, and it was certainly intimidating, but by now I had found my voice: I knew what I could do.

I wanted to show my gratitude but in a way that would make the audience smile. I was speaking on a rostrum of greats so I began, 'My brothers and sisters, African-American brothers and sisters, you need to know that there are Black brothers and sisters in the UK and right across Europe who will not believe me when I tell them that I'm here in Atlanta at the State of the Black World Conference, and my warm-up acts are: the civil rights leader Reverend Jesse Jackson, the civil rights leader Al Sharpton, California congresswoman Maxine Waters, Martin Luther King III …'

This drew huge laughter, huge applause. Here was this young activist from London embracing the big stage. Even my heroes had to smile.

I had made my mark and set the foundation for what would

become a decades-long and incredibly inspiring connection with leading figures within the African-American civil rights movement. The conference really helped me make a name for myself on the other side of the pond, which then meant that, coming home, I could call upon some of these big names when it came to collaborations. Which was to prove of huge benefit to our mission at Operation Black Vote.

The first person I hit up was Reverend Al Sharpton, who accepted an invitation from me to host a tour of the UK in January 2001. Sharpton had been to the UK before, some five or six years earlier, when Lee Jasper had invited him over to highlight the killing of fifteen-year-old Rolan Adams, who'd been murdered by a gang of white racists in South London in 1991. Sharpton had consequently become a big supporter of Rolan's mother, Audrey Adams, who was now campaigning with Lee.

Sharpton agreed to come, but with provisos. First, unlike when we brought over Emanuel Cleaver and he flew economy class, Sharpton's representative said, 'Look, he'll come, and he doesn't want any money, but he needs to fly at least business class. It's nothing to do with the money, it's to do with being ready to work.'

To fly in economy was about £500; to fly in business was £5,000 and to fly first class back then was £10,000. I thought, *how am I going to do this?* There have been countless times as an activist when I've had to think creatively, ask for favours and hustle to get things done, to achieve our aims, and this was certainly one of them.

I had a good friend who worked for British Airways called Keith Kerr, who later stood as the Lib Dem candidate in an Uxbridge by-election, but back then was a senior executive with BA. So I called him up and turned on the charm.

'Keith, can you do me a really big favour? I'm flying over Reverend Al Sharpton, and I want to fly with British Airways, but we need to get an upgrade for him to business class …'

'Leave it to me,' Keith said. Later that day, he called me back to say he'd got the Reverend his upgrade but there was a catch: if the plane was full and BA were short on business seats or first-class seats, Sharpton would have to be demoted back to economy. I knew that was too big a risk to take.

'I can't have that as a potential embarrassment,' I explained. 'He has to be guaranteed business class otherwise can you imagine the embarrassment? Al Sharpton showing up at the airport for a business class seat, only to be told, "Sorry, sir, there are no seats left. You'll have to go back to economy." He's going to turn around and go home or give me a hard time. Either way, I don't want that.'

'All right,' Keith said. 'Look, I didn't tell you this but call this number …'

It was a bucket shop – a discount travel agent – in Southall, West London.

'If you go via Air India, you'll get a first-class ticket for just a couple of thousand pounds.'

So I took Keith's advice, made some phone calls and got a first-class ticket for a knockdown price. Deal done!

I called the media: press, TV, radio, the works. The ratpack was waiting for the Reverend at Arrivals when he landed. All the other travellers stopped and looked quizzically, but when Reverend Al – 'Big Al' in those days – appeared, the flashbulbs started going and the hacks hounded him with questions, and he just breezed through it like it was a walk in the park. Clearly he was used to attention and he liked it.

'This guy Woolley knows how to put on a show,' Sharpton said as he rocked up with his entourage.

'Reverend Sharpton, how was everything?' I said, beaming.

'We're good, we're good. Everything's all good. Good hotel. Good itinerary …'

'Excellent, Reverend Sharpton. And how was the flight?'

Sharpton stopped, touched my arm and peered over his glasses.

'Put it this way, Brother Woorleee,' – this was how he pronounced my name – 'We landed.'

As I travelled around the country with Reverend Sharpton, I watched how he performed, how he spoke, how he never used notes. He just had this gift. It was remarkable to see first-hand. Once, he spoke to a group of teenagers in Peckham, some of whom had been thrown out of school and ended up in pupil referral units. He stood in front of them, looked them all in the eye and said, 'Let me tell you this: if I knock you down, that's on me. But if I come back a week later and you're still on the ground, that's on you.' Wow! It was simple rhetoric but you could see the words having an impact on this young audience. Sharpton, like his mentee the Revd Jesse Jackson, is a master wordsmith, with the perfect delivery of tone and tenor.

Our big stage event was at Church House in London, packed with about two thousand people. The Reverend was on fire. He was loving them and they were adoring him. No written speech, just a handful of notes that he barely used. The apprentice Woolley was in listen-and-learn mode.

Afterwards Sharpton said to me, 'Brother Woorleeee, you have something really special here. In the US, we would not have had an audience like you have assembled here tonight – Africans, Asians, Caribbeans, white people all together listening to a message about race equality. We can learn from you. Hold onto that because that'll be your strength.'

* * *

We brought over the Reverend Jesse Jackson in 2005, his entourage was double that of Sharpton's. The Reverend Jesse Jackson was – is – African-American royalty.

This was the man who worked with and marched with the greatest civil rights leader in our history, Dr Martin Luther King. And in many ways he took on the mantle after King was assassinated. I never knew him in the 80s when he twice ran for President, but I saw him on TV. There was nothing like him before and nothing like him since. He was a tall, athletic, fast-talking politician and preacher – and he was Black.

The 1990 Trust's director, Karen Chouhan who, like me, is from Leicester, is a very dynamic activist, and a brilliant speaker too. She and her team, including Audrey Adams, organised a national tour. We, OBV, were the junior partners on the tour. Think about this for a second: activists with little or no money managed to get a bus, get it emblazoned with a wraparound picture of the great man – designed of course by Jon Daniel – and off we'd go, travelling around the country, holding rallies about ending racism in our lifetime and empowering communities. It was an incredible learning experience for me and great exposure – as a civil rights icon, Reverend Jackson must have been on every news report. I'm guessing it's like being in a rock band on tour. On the coach you're sitting chatting, or sleeping, then when you arrive, it's showtime. And the Reverend Jackson was the main attraction.

I am very proud of the great many things we did together during that time. I remember it fondly but it also exhausted me completely. Big players like Sharpton and Jackson expect a slick operation, packed houses and media at every juncture. But our team took the challenge and ran with it. Jesse Jackson was brilliant, encouraging but demanding. It was as though he'd chosen me to be his protégé … I was honoured.

These were tremendous experiences and it felt like very exciting times for Operation Black Vote and all the things we were trying to achieve. On a personal note, I was able to learn so much from being around these great campaigners, just watching how they 'performed'. I've been extremely lucky because I've learned from some of the best Black orators, both in the US and in the UK.

What I came to realise is that you can cherry-pick the things that might work for you but you must wrap it up in your style. I learned very early on from Sharpton and Jackson not to read from a script because no matter how good you are, you must look an audience right in the eye. Sure, without one in front of you, you make a few mistakes or you forget things, but it's infinitely better than reading verbatim from a script. Stand-up comedians, preachers, great politicians – anyone who's selling an idea – must look at the audience and engage with it. What the best speakers in the world do is speak to an audience of thousands as though they're speaking to you as an individual. They're looking at you, they're pointing at you, they're smiling, laughing, engaging with you. I also learned from these people not to talk about what you don't know. And to have facts at your disposal but don't be a fact machine. Tell stories, tell *your* story and speak to people's hearts and minds rather than mouthing some corny script. By watching great orators I learned it is about making an emotional connection. Emotion, as well as two-thirds of human communication being non-verbal, is what gives deeper meaning to your words.

Everyone has their own strategy, but my own modus operandi has always been to seek to better understand the opposition and ask myself: how can I can take them on the journey I want them to go on rather than try to crush my opponent simply to get my own way or massage my own ego?

I once watched Jesse Jackson spend ten minutes of his forty-minute speech thanking people, bringing them on stage and letting them get the applause. Another time, in Chicago, he stopped the show and said, 'Can you bring out the kitchen staff, please? Can you bring out the porters?' He waited until all the staff who people so often walk by, barely giving any attention to, had come on stage to be thanked. 'These are the people who keep this place running,' he said. 'These are the people who make sure you're fed, who make sure that you're well looked after. These are my brothers and sisters.' The place just went wild. These thank you's would set the tone. They would remind us why we do what we do. But even more than that, for those people he brought on stage, for every person's hand that he shook – they felt a million dollars. An act of simple generosity they would never forget.

The first quarter of all the Reverend Jackson speeches was about showcasing others – I guess it was his succession planning. I learned from him that you must make sure that you're bringing up other people so they know that they have a big role to play. He did this to me several times in front of big audiences. He said, 'Brother Simon Woolley, can you come up on stage, please?' And then he said, 'Brothers and sisters, you see this brother right here? If Dr Martin Luther King was around today, this brother would be in his team.'

Above: Here I'm seven or eight years old, in class at Taylor Street School. A natty dresser, even then!

Left: With my foster mum Pippi and my older foster brother Mick. Next to us is Pippi's daughter Pat, and her daughter Mary, who's also on the front cover of this book.

Right: At the launch of Operation Black Vote in July 1996. I'm second from the right.

Above: Campaigning at Brixton Market in 2002. © *Martin Godwin/Guardian/eyevine*

Below: At a rally for the Reverend Jesse Jackson, Birmingham 2014.

Left: With the Reverend Al Sharpton at the House of Lords seminar on Stop and Search in 2020.

Right: With Marvin Rees, outside the British Embassy in Washington D.C.

Below: At the launch of the Race Disparity Unit in October 2017.

Above: With Tanmanjeet Singh Desai MP, Helen Grant MP, Dr Rami Ranger CBE and Speaker of the House John Bercow at the launch of the OBV Shadowing Scheme at Speaker's House on 18 January 2018.

Diversity UK Image © Lopa Patel

Above: With David Lammy MP at the launch of the Green Park BAME 100 Board Talent Index, in October 2017.

© PA Images / Alamy Stock Photo

Right: With Naomi Campbell in No. 10, waiting to speak with PM Theresa May to talk about Africa Fashion Aid, 15 May 2018.

Here are just two of the incredible ads that Saatchi & Saatchi created in conjunction with Operation Black Vote. Above is our re-creation of that infamous photo of the Bullingdon Club in Oxford, but here with BAME people looking as if they were born to rule. Below, David Harewood agreed to do whiteface for a vote urging BAME people to register to vote.

What a day! 10 October 2019, the day that Simon Woolley, a boy from the St Matthew's estate in Leicester, was knighted by the Queen. *Top left: © Yui Mok/ PA Images / Alamy Stock Photo. Top right: © PA Images / Alamy Stock Photo*

To the left is a picture of me and my son Luca, who stole the limelight – and my medal! – at Buckingham Palace.

Above: With my sponsors Baroness Meral Hussein-Ece and Baroness Lola Young, when I was inducted to the House of Lords on 21 October, 2019.

Below: As one of my first acts as principal at Homerton College, Cambridge, it was my honour to grant my friend and mentor, the Reverend Jesse Jackson, a fellowship of the college on 14 December, 2021. © *Homerton College/David Johnson.*

Above: The night before Barbados was to become a republic on 30 November 2021, I dined with HRH Prince Charles, the British High Commissioner Scott Furssedonn-Wood, and his wife Elizabeth. Here we are with the chefs.

Above: 1 October 2021. The vice-principal formally inducts me as principal of Homerton College, Cambridge.

© *Homerton College/David Johnson.*

Right: I was told this cloak would give me superhuman powers. I can't fly, but I'm sure I can do great things here.

Is there a better accolade? Can you imagine the Reverend Jesse Jackson putting his arm around you and saying that? It was an incredible feeling and goes to show that the real greats use their platforms to champion other people, to lift up those coming up behind them, and not just to preach their own ideas.

Sharpton, Jackson and Maxine Waters are the real barn-stormers but in complete contrast, I also watched Trevor Phillips' manner and learned from that. His style is to adopt a quiet and a thoughtful tone, which has the effect of making him sound utterly reasonable and incredibly knowledgeable, and thus convincing. With his deep, measured tone he'd always comes across as plausible and he was acutely aware that for change to happen, he had to convince powerful white people that he should be listened to. And they did, still do. In sharp contrast, Black activists such as Lee Jasper or Bernie Grant spoke to their Black audience first and foremost in a vernacular and passion that demanded action.

And then there was this up-and-coming guy called Barack Obama, who was just breaking through in a big way. The Reverend Jesse Jackson invited me to a Rainbow push coalition event in 2006, in Chicago, when all the presidential hopefuls were there. That was the power of Jackson.

Despite being the new kid on the block, Obama was already hitting the campaign trail hard and was being touted as a serious contender, not just for the Democratic nomination but also maybe to become president outright. Watching him was a revelation. He was by no means a preacher in the Sharpton or Jackson mould; there was no table thumping and no call and response, he was more of a political raconteur-rhetorician – a wonderful storyteller who wove each of his narratives quietly but passionately into an overarching message, taking us all to a better place. And in this abstract 'place' you found a sense of belonging that was empowering and rewarding. That was the Obama message, a message that would become crystallised by two words 'hope' and 'change', and find expression in the political slogan to end all political slogans: 'Yes we can!'

When the US election rolled around on 4 November 2008, we organised a fantastic election night party in the Café de Paris club in the West End, thanks to Winsome Grace-Cornish, who knew the manager or the owner. It was the hottest ticket in town. We had members of the Labour Cabinet fighting to get a ticket; I remember some senior politicians were outside being made to queue, calling me up to get them in. I simply explained that they would have to wait in line – this was the people's party and the usual special privileges didn't apply. It was a magical night. Everybody gave a speech, but alas we had to close at 3am, an hour before the big announcement was made. Though we knew by then that it was going our way.

In a number of speeches I would give post-election I would talk about how Obama taught me to aim higher than I'd been doing. If someone had said to me in 2006, 'Mr Woolley, I'll do you a deal, here right now. Sign here and I promise I'll guarantee that we'll make history and deliver the first African-American … Vice President', then I'd have replied, to my shame, 'Where do I sign?' We'd been conditioned not only to settle for less, but to be grateful for that. Barack Obama taught us with his and Jackson's audacity of hope that we can aim for the top.

Then at the inauguration in January 2009 we had another party at Skylon, a designer chic, neo-1950s style restaurant encased in floor-to-ceiling windows that overlooks the Thames. It's like something out of *Mad Men*. David Cameron came, as well as the American Embassy team. My dear friend Sue Wedlake confided in me that, after the awful Bush years, 'We've never been so loved.' That felt like a new exciting dawn for all of us. I never tired of saying that, finally, there was a Black man in the White House. As wonderful as that time was, and we rode that crest of a wave for months, we never allowed ourselves to believe we were living in a post-racial world, as some suggested. We were also very much aware that Obama did not have the luxury to be a race radical president. Even a moderate, decent Black president like Obama would unleash a strain of race hatred that took all of us by surprise. For some the existence of white America was under threat, or at least that's how it was portrayed. As a result the Tea Party movement was born, which would wage a personal war against Obama and ultimately spawn its white knight – I'm choosing my words very carefully here – Donald Trump.

* * *

Through Sharpton and Jackson, and their support teams including the remarkably effective quiet man and mad Chelsea supporter James Gomez, we've all become very close friends. Whenever they would come into the UK, I'd be the first to know. 'OK, Brother Woolley, we're in town to do this that or that other, but what else are we going to do while we're there?'

For example, in 2015 the Reverend Al Sharpton visited again, finishing up a whistle-stop tour of the UK with an address to the Oxford Union. By then he had done so much for us that I felt we needed to celebrate with a special night, to give thanks for his ongoing sterling efforts as well as our professional and personal bond. And if I could throw in a bit of the ol' London town razzamatazz that Americans are such suckers for at the same time, so much the better!

I called up my friend, the wonderful Alan Edwards, PR guru to many stars, including our mutual friend Naomi Campbell.

'Alan, I need a place to host Reverend Sharpton. Somewhere, well, swanky.'

'Leave it to me.'

Alan got back to me just a couple of hours later. 'I've got you the Groucho Club. And they're going to wine and dine you and your guests. No charge.'

'Alan, you're a legend!'

We had about twenty guests, including the actor Colin Salmon, the singer and actor Beverley Knight, and Nero

Ughwujabo, who a couple of years later would become a special advisor to No.10. It was a wonderful, wonderful evening. The champagne flowed and Sharpton was animated as ever. It was a moment to celebrate but also another way of solidifying and recognising the links between Black Britain and Black America.

Sharpton would say, 'When I come to London, Woolley's my man.' And when I went to the States, Sharpton was my man, along with the Reverend Jesse Jackson. But such deep-rooted, empathic connections are never just about policy, global change-making, thought leadership or cutting deals. Or, on a personal level, hanging out with peers and heroes whose company always feels like something of an indulgence. It wasn't even about impressing 'the man' or proving that Black activists and leaders scrub up just as well as anyone else.

No, the metanarrative to these gatherings was about challenging a canard that Black people don't get along with each other, that we are inherently distrustful of each other, tribal, or too easily manipulated by third parties. The notion that Black people can't get along and thus cannot achieve collaborative success is a falsehood, a lie and a dangerous trope which, left unchallenged, encourages a lack of confidence, a lack of ambition and a resignation that is the antithesis of Obama's 'Yes we can' clarion call for success. Short of systemic racism, it is the greatest obstacle Black people face in terms of personal growth and collective development, which is why I'm so passionate about celebrating not just what Black people can do for each other, but what we can do for other cultures across the globe.

What I like about their relationship with the US, the UK and Black British politics is that the mutual respect means that if you're with them, they will showcase you, so when Jesse Jackson steps up and the lights are flashing and the crowds are listening to him, hanging on his every word, he will say: 'Brothers and sisters, ladies and gentlemen, I need to tell you about our European brothers and sisters who are my guests and are doing what we do.' In France, in London, in Berlin, and one by one, he would introduce us to the audience. Now, I've been a little bit accustomed to this because I've seen it before with him. But for people like Helen Grant – Operation Black Vote alumni, and the first conservative female of African descent to be elected on the conservative benches – she'd never seen this before. In fact, when you're brought up in the North of England and, you live that kind of sheltered space, not around Black people, for her to be around our brothers and sisters. She told me afterwards that it was a life-changing moment, one in which she was much more fully aware of who she truly was.

CHAPTER 7

WHITE LIBERALS, BLACK CONSERVATIVES AND ALLIES

Operation Black Vote has always been a non-partisan organisation, right from the beginning. This is absolutely key to so much of what we have achieved and helped us to succeed in many areas where others have failed. Our first Chair at the time, Lee Jasper was wedded to Labour, as is our present Chair, Rita Patel, a Labour Party councillor. Both our instinct and experience with the Labour Party, which I'll explore later, led us to take up a strategy that looked back then counter-intuitive. In 1996, when we started, Thatcher's shadow still loomed large around and 90 per cent of Black voters supported Labour. Our antennae knew that for real change we needed all politicians from all sides to fight for the Black vote.

Our non-partisan approach meant we could – at least in theory – work with any gatekeeper who could help open doors that would translate into tackling systemic race inequality. We absolutely felt that putting all our political eggs in the Labour Party basket meant that the Labour Party could take us even more for granted than they were already doing – 'Where else you going to go, right?' was the prevailing attitude – but also we couldn't be so easily dismissed by those on the Right. I mean, you need look no further than the way the Right, including some prominent Conservatives, vilify and simplify their attack on the Black Lives Matter movement. BLM, for example, has been regularly accused of being a 'bunch of communists' – a lazy yet sometimes effective tool that is used to shut down debate and block change.

And if we turn our gaze to the US, particularly under Donald Trump, the Republican Party has often had little or nothing to say to African-Americans, and Latinos (with the exception of the Cuban Latinos, whose historical hatred of the Left and Fidel Castro found a home within the Republican movement), not least because, well, they're never going to vote for them. In the UK, however, our notion of Black politics isn't so narrow. In fact, the idea of Africans, Caribbeans, Asians and other minority ethnic communities being politically homogenous is more than offensive.

The big question for us as we set out to transform politics was how do we convince the parties, particularly the Conservatives, that there's a political dividend to being inclusive and speaking to and for our communities? Mission impossible, right? Wrong. Actually the pitch couldn't have been easier.

Take religion. It is by its very nature conservative with a small c. And who mostly subscribes to religion in the UK? Right, you got it in one! Those Black, Asian and minority communities. Whether it's the church, the mosque, the gurdwara or the temple, the people going through the doors in great numbers are Black and Asian, which often means they are socially conservative.

Children and parents of the Commonwealth also had a Left-leaning strand born from our histories that have been shaped by the colonial experience, a working-class background and no doubt the new immigrant lived experience with all its frothing racism that our parents encountered. Those civil rights movements we started or joined were rooted in social justice and racial justice, which for many of us in a political space was the Left.

So you can see these two competing tensions – socially conservative, politically Labour – because they offered some respect, decency and above all, rights.

This obvious tension was also an opportunity to tell a truth, a fundamental truth that would help them, the competing political parties, to see the value in courting the Black vote.

* * *

I don't think I met William Hague when he was Leader of the Conservative Party. I'm sure I'd remember. But I am sure that I met his 'people', who had seen what noise we made during the election, and they were keen to understand what we were about and was there anything in it for them.

I set out our store, crystal clear: OBV was non-partisan. Our goal was for government and society to acknowledge and effectively tackle deep-seated race inequality. They, the Conservatives, should talk about that, and be more representative. The prize, I offered, would win them crucial Black votes. Moreover, I argued, with much data at my fingertips, these votes would be in key marginal seats.

'Look,' I'd say, 'who goes to church more than anyone else? What other ethnic groups are deeply religious, socially conservative?' Yes, I'd answer for them, our communities: African, Caribbean, Indian, Pakistani, Bangladeshi, Turkish, and more. 'So ask yourself but one question,' I quizzed – I'd seen the then barrel-chested civil rights agitator the Reverend Al Sharpton use the rhetoric device with great dramatic effect, with his one finger pointing to heaven – 'why do you think that these deeply religious, socially conservative communities, who agree with you on the big issues – family, education, law and order – barely think of voting for you?'

My rhetorical question tended to be met with silence, to which I duly obliged, 'Well, I'll tell you why. It's because they think you're a bunch of racists and when they look at your policies and the representation in your Party, they will say, "Nah! Are you kidding me? They don't like us, they don't want us and they'll use the most powerful levers of the state – the police – to make our lives a misery.'"

I'd just hit them with an Exocet missile, the job now was to give them hope.

'Here's the thing,' I'd explain, 'you won't have to do an enormous amount to begin to get traction, but you do have to mean it and deliver it. Talk about the gross inequalities and have a plan to deal with it; shout about the contributions our communities have made, and not just the entrepreneurial Indian shopkeeper, important as they are. You need to know there are a lot of Black closet Tories, and or wannabe Tories. And finally, have Black and Asian faces in winnable seats.'

I was narrating the script for a modern Tory Party and officials clearly scribbled notes with much enthusiasm.

Here you might say: 'Let me get this right. How come you, Simon Woolley and Operation Black Vote, who were in essence a bunch of activist volunteers who'd been on the scene for about five minutes, were steering the Conservative Party on a journey of no return?' Fair question, to which I don't have a gilt-edge answer, but it's true. That's what did. I think timing is everything. Tony Blair had just given the Tories a kicking from which they might not recover, ever. He had a majority like no other. And no leading political figure was more charismatic than Blair in his pomp. One could speculate that if his ego hadn't gone to his head, particularly when he pledged his lot with President George

Bush to go to war to non-existent nuclear weapons in Iraq, he could have made a pact with the Liberal Democrats, introduced proportional representation, and the Tory Party as we know it would not exist.

So, given what they were confronting around the turn of the century, the Tories were looking for ways to claw back credibility, and to lose the label that has recently come back to haunt them, that they are the 'nasty party', a party that has no regard for the poor and panders to prejudice that knowingly sows deep division. Our little but strategic focused organisation offered in part a Tory reset for the twenty-first century.

* * *

Although I ran OBV on a daily basis, Lee Jasper was our leader and figurehead. Jasper, like me, had been a street hustler; sharp-minded, fast-talking and – unlike me – took no shit. I enjoyed his political acumen, particularly at that time. He'd often sit me down and say 'Son,' – he's only a few years older than me but it was used as a term of endearment – 'Son, let me tell about some of these enlightened Conservatives, in contrast with so-called progressive Liberals. A pragmatic One Nation Conservative, who is progressive in their thinking, will be the first to say, "I know there's a problem, and, frankly, I'm not going to pretend I know how to effectively fix it. Can you help?" In contrast, the attitude on the Left and among the Liberal elite is too often that "We're the drivers of social justice. We know what we're doing, we understand tackling racial justice as well if not better than you, so just leave things to us.'"

That, Lee said, was why that for all the talk and taking of the moral high ground over the Conservatives, the promised big shifts in tackling systemic race inequality never occurred. (Though for all that Lee would talk about being non-partisan, he couldn't help himself calling the Tories a bunch of nasty racists now and again.)

Looking back, it is incredible how this small band of activists had this multi-pronged strategy to push the now all-powerful Labour, with, I might add, little success. The word was that some big Labour Party hitters viewed the broader civil society organisations such as Liberty, Amnesty and Charter 88 – and that would include us – as 'whingers'. Couldn't we be grateful for the democratic reform agenda the Party was delivering?

We never got crushed by knock-backs, but that's not say it didn't hurt. I remember a meeting with the then Labour Party Cabinet Minister Harriet Harman and EU Minister Keith Vaz.

In the run-up to one election, they promised me that more Black candidates would fight winnable seats. But in the end, after the fierce horse-trading they had to do with their financial backers the Unions, Black people lost out. Every single time we picked ourselves up and kept marching forward, taking steps in the right direction.

It was undoubtedly twenty years of persistence and

building friendships on both side – not matey, drinks-in-the-pub type friendships, but friendships where you trust each other, despite your disagreements. It was that friendship in which the Conservative Prime Minister Theresa May set up and announced the world's first political Race Disparity Audit to identify what she described as 'burning injustices' in society.

The Left didn't like that Operation Black Vote was meeting Conservatives either. I once had a meeting with Michael Howard, once described by one of his colleagues, as 'something dark', about the rise of the British National Party in seats like Burnley and Stoke. I said to him that part of the problem was that the Conservative councils didn't contest these northern areas because they wrote them off as a Labour stronghold – 'As a result,' I told him, 'removing yourselves as a voting option herds bigots and right-wingers to the hands of the BNP. You need to be there. Even if you can't win, you'll stop the BNP.' I convinced Howard to go to Burnley, give an anti-BNP speech and put candidates in winnable seats so they could take Burnley and outflank the BNP.

Labour was incandescent with rage; so much so that when I arrived at the Labour Party Conference, within five minutes of being there, a minister – I don't want to mention his name – gave me such a dressing-down. 'What the fuck are you doing dealing with Michael Howard?' he exploded. 'The guy is a wretch, he's a dog, he's a xenophobe – and you've been dealing with him? Simon, you need to think about what you're doing because a lot of us are deeply disappointed in you.'

He spoke to me like I was a little kid in front of all his mandarins. I was shaking with rage and embarrassment, but I did say, 'Unlike you, we in the Black community don't have luxury of choosing perfect friends. And that is doubly so when dealing with the BNP.'

I took the humiliation on the chin, but I resolved that no one in politics or anywhere else would speak to me in that way again. To me, this was another example of the white liberal elite, telling Black people what was best for us and how politics should be, above all solely on their terms.

For Black activists, taking on the BNP and their poisonous ideology was much more than fighting bigots and thugs, important as that is. In big political terms they were not serious players; wherever they went – they only got into local government – they were found to be incompetent legislators. But the disproportionate airtime they received poisoned the political well, giving voice to chancers and ideologues such as Nigel Farage, and finding a home in mainstream parties for followers of the BNP, and to some extent legitimising their xenophobia that would prove difficult to effectively combat.

Calling out racist bigots such as BNP head Nick Griffin and Tommy Robinson is always exhausting, but relatively easy. Give them enough rope and they'll pretty much do the job for you. Our multifaceted challenge for greater race equality has been to take on thugs, thwart the Right, and sometimes the Left, from pandering to prejudice for short-term gain, and then point out that the liberal elite has in part failed to fundamentally dismantle structural racism because it always claims that they 'know best'.

* * *

The inescapable truth for system change to occur means that you need pressure on the outside and warriors on the inside. This is why Operation Black Vote made 'political representation' one of our three fundamental pillars of what we were trying to achieve. We need people of colour in the Cabinet offices, party central offices, as well as the courtrooms and the council chambers. We have long understood that you just can't sit around and wait for people to come along with enlightened views without your involvement, your insight, and above all, your lived experiences. We've known that the political structures that have often kept us out, and not served us as well we'd like, can change, but it's us who must be the drivers of change.

A lot of people in the Westminster bubble think that I started work with Theresa May around 2013, when the 'Go home' vans shamed her and the UK government. It's true, that moment added more intensity, that began with my fury, my questioning, 'OK, what does real Conservative change look like?' But I have to say it began way before, while the Conservaties were in opposition, and the Tories we desperately trying to claw back ground.

A team of Conservatives got together and began to try to

change the Party. Theresa May was probably their loudest cheerleader, telling anyone who'd listen that the Tory Party must change, particularly their 'nasty party' image.

This might be hard to imagine but I remember a working lunch at my friend Iqbal Wahhab's restaurant The Cinnamon Club, one of the top places to dine in London at the time. This was where Theresa May sat down to break bread with the me, senior officials and Lee Jasper. I suspect both of them are happy that I can longer find the picture of them deep in conversation, but trust me, it happened.

After speaking with us, their plan was simple: find high-flying, talented Black and Asian individuals and they would do the rest. And to their credit, they did.

Theresa May would say to me, 'Simon, I know you're wedded to all-Black short lists but that's not the Tory way. We'll do it, but our way.'

And their way was quite extraordinary, but, I have to say, effective. It went something like this: find someone extremely able – lawyer, businessman or -woman – someone who looks like a Tory if it wasn't for their skin colour. And then get our own big political beasts to tell the local Party that he or she would be a wonderful asset. They knew from bitter experience that you can't just parachute someone in with a blue rosette and the job is done. The election defeat of the safe Conservative seat of Cheltenham in 1992 was a chastening experience, when the Conservative local party chair let it be known that they'd sooner have a white Lib Dem MP than a Black Conservative. And they meant it. The posh Black barrister John Taylor lost the safe seat to a Lib Dem, stating his loss had nothing to do with race. OK, John!

Having learned from that Cheltenham experience, the inner team knew that you had to win local members over first so this time they prepared a charm offensive so the locals would believe it was their choice. That's when the breakthrough occurred: trailblazers such as my dear friends Adam Afriyie and Shailesh Vara really began the unstoppable surge for Black and Asian Tories. So by the time Theresa May was in Government we'd already had a backstory, that we never really spoke about, but it was one of trust.

But I do remember the summer of when Theresa May's Special Advisor Nick Timothy called me up for a meeting about the 'Go Home' vans. He asked to meet him outside the Home Office so that we could chat privately.

We're both from the Midlands, and football crazy, so we hit it off. I didn't share his passion for cricket, but two out three ain't bad. I told him bluntly, 'Doesn't matter what you say, you fucked up with the vans. All those years of you saying you're no longer the nasty party and then this.'

Timothy's defence was that actually it wasn't Theresa May's decision but another minister's, but she accepted that she had to carry the can.

Now, when you're in these situations where you know you've got your opponent on the ropes you can go for the knockout line: 'I knew you were a bunch of racists, and you haven't changed', and you can go a step further and let the press know you've told the Tories that too. Or you can take a different tack.

Nick asked me how they could come back from this. This was one of those moments where the fifteen-year history of trust comes to the fore. Three things sprang immediately to mind. 'If you want to show that the government understands,' I said, 'then do something about "Stop and Search". They are just rounding up Black kids for fun. It's not Stop and Search, it's stop and humiliate. And then there are the deaths in police custody. You need to speak to the families.' I pointed behind me, to the multi-coloured building of the Home Office. 'Nick,' I said, 'everything that comes out these offices is bad news for Black people: policing, immigration, prisons. Undertake a race equality policy audit, lay it bare, be honest. Then find solutions. I promise you, Nick, you do this, all the other departments will have to follow suit.' To my utter surprise, he not only didn't baulk but thought these were great ideas. And he would take it back to the boss.

Those conversations precipitated a number of actions in which the Home Secretary would challenge both her own department's and police practices that deeply prejudiced Black people's lives, namely Stop and Search, and Black deaths in police custody.

The first time I saw it in action was when I was called to the Home Office meeting with the Home Secretary and police chiefs. I can picture the scene now: There was an oblong table, on one side were senior Police chiefs, all male, all white, headed by the then Met Head, Bernard Hogan-

Howe. They looked intimidating in their uniforms bestrewn with badges of seniority that left you in no doubt that this was the Met top brass.

On the other side of the table sat the Home Secretary, her advisors, along with white officials and a small number of Black activists. The subject was 'Stop and Search' and its impact on the Black community. The police presented their case with diagrams of 'Crime hotspots', backed up with the claim that 'our offices are extremely professional and never discriminate'. May listened impassively, then turned to Hogan-Howe and said as blunt as you like: 'I respectfully disagree. My calculations are that about one third of Stop and Searches are as near as damn it, illegal, and as such, instead of building trust, you're losing it. I demand better from our police officers.'

I couldn't believe that a Conservative Home Secretary, from a Party who normally prides themselves on being on the side of the police regardless of the facts, was giving the Met's top brass a dressing-down, and in front of me. I remember thinking, *Go, girl, let them have it with both barrels!*

Hogan-Howe and his colleagues fidgeted with the folders before saying something to the effect of, 'Our officers always try and improve our performances', before ending the meeting.

May had put them on notice with the clear warning that if the numbers didn't change, Section 60, which was the most blunt and overused tool in the police's box, that could be deplored as a dragnet and around hundreds of Black youths to 'Stop, Search and Humiliate' could be taken away from them.

The other police area that May chose to worry about was Black deaths in police custody. The Home Secretary had gone out of her way to listen to family members who had lost loved ones in police custody. She was struck by their harrowing stories, many of which were exacerbated by the fact that some of individuals needed mental health practitioners, rather than heavy-handed officers with the inevitable tragic outcome.

May enlisted Black Mental Health UK Limited Director Matilda Macattram and Black mental health organisations to hold conferences around the country, educating both the police and mental health practitioners about their failings in how they deal with Black communities and mental health.

These areas that I worked directly and indirectly with May helped build trust between us. We acknowledged we had many differences, not least around immigration and drugs policy, but we could park those and work on what we did agree on.

In the end my idea for a Race Equality Audit in the Home Office got kicked into the long grass, not least because I was told that Prime Minister David Camerion didn't like it. He wanted to put his race equality 'eggs' in his pet project: 'End Racism by 2020'. A project that one of his advisors in Downing Street told me when I asked what did that look like, dryly responded, 'Not very much, Simon. Don't raise your hopes.'

The dumping of the Race Audit and the empty vessel that was 'End Racism by 2020' did not knock me or anyone of our team. We asked, even demanded a lot from the political establishment, but could not afford to be crestfallen when little or nothing was given.

Our time did come, and in extraordinary circumstances too. Cameron had lost the Brexit vote and he knew he had to resign. In the dog fight to become PM, Boris Johnson and Michael Gove knocked each other out, which allowed Theresa May to saunter into No.10 uncontested.

If you remember, May's last few years as home secretary, confronting race inequality, then you'd not be surprised by her 'Burning injustices' speech when she took office.

She was only about three months into the job when her special advisor called me out of the blue and said, 'Simon, you know that idea you had about the Race Equality Audit?'

Do I remember? I thought, *Of course I do. I remember you kicking into the long grass.* 'Yeah, are you going to bring it back?'

'No,' he said. 'We're going much further with it and undertaking an audit right across all government departments.'

I couldn't believe what I was hearing. I thought, *This is a potentially a very big deal*, but refused myself to do cartwheels. My first thought was how would government ministers and senior civil servants translate the facts into action. Equally, I was petrified that malicious people would use the data that was there and manipulate it to work against us. Because, if you cherry pick the data, then it can be spun in a malicious way. For example, take knife crime in the capital with the shocking and disproportionate number of young Black men being stabbed and dying. I was petrified the data could be maliciously spun to suggest there's something within Black DNA that is somehow violent, because individuals are killing each other from our communities. Instead of looking at this through a public health lens that is a kaleidoscope of determinants, it becomes seen through a narrow prisim of 'its only a Black community problem'.

The truth is that when Europe's knife crime centre was in Glasgow, Scotland, nobody associated race with those knife crimes. Furthermore, Glasgow began to effectively deal with its knife and gang problem by tackling it as a public health challenge. For that reason, I was worried about how the data would be used. Thankfully, my fears did not come to fruition, at least during May's term in office.

They took about a year to gather all the information across Whitehall departments and they called it the Race Disparity Unit, headed up by the very able Marcus Bell and a team of twenty-five collecting the data and then making sense of it. I, along with about dozen people, was on the advisory group, pointing out where the gaps were and advising about the pitfalls. I'd also regularly meet with the minister in charge of overseeing the project, Cabinet Secretary Ben Gummer. He later told me that he'd done a lot things in government, but this project, he said, '*your* project, I'm particularly proud of.'

May was riding high and thought that if she went to the polls, she'd get an even bigger majority, but that didn't quite go to plan, and to make matters worse, the Labour leader Jeremy Corbyn nearly did the impossible, reigniting the Black vote with some assistance from hip-hop star Stormzy in swing seats such as Croydon South and Kensington. One of the victims of those inner-city seats that swung to Labour was Gavin Barwell, a good man, a decent man, who lost his seat in Croydon Central – a 40 per cent Black electorate – to Labour's Sarah Jones. Barwell joined May as her new chief of staff, replacing Nick Timothy, who had to be sacrificed for the near electoral loss. Barwell convinced May that they had to redouble their efforts to regain areas such as Croydon and show that 'One Nation' Conservatives could reach out to all parts of society, including the disadvantaged, Black and white.

As part of their grand plan, Barwell brought in Nero Ughwujabo, a Croydon race equality campaigner who was respected nationally. I'd known and worked with Nero for many years and so was not surprised when he called me to ask my opinion as to whether or not he should take the job as the nation's first Black policy special advisor to the Prime Minister. 'Nero,' I said, 'are you kidding me? You have to take this job, but on one condition: own it, make it yours and think big.' Nero didn't need my advice, he just wanted a sounding board from a trusted friend, but he did, indeed, own that space in a humble but mission-led way. It obviously would also assist me too: Nick Timothy was gone, but my old friend was now catapulted into the heart of government at No.10. I thought Nero and I could dramatically move the race equality dial in a way that had never been done before.

Although Timothy had left, we still had regular conversations about the progress of the Race Disparty Unit. We both agreed that the Brexit mess and the demand of the hardline Brexiteers, Jacob Rees-Mogg, Boris Johnson and Michael Gove, had the potential to drain the life blood from normal day-to-day politics. I feared that with the PM being sucked into Brexit warfare, the potential for the Race Disparity Audit to drive change would lose its momentum. Timothy agreed. 'So, Simon, what's your grand plan?' he said. 'Spit it out.'

'I drive the change across Whitehall using the Race Disparity data. I chair a group of advisors and I troubleshoot across the departments using the mantra coined by David Lammy in his review of racism in the criminal justice system: "Explain the disparities or change".'

He replied, 'Have you asked for that role? No? Well, ask.'

He set up a meeting with JoJo Penn – now Baroness Penn, but then a senior advisor working for May – and May's new key Special Advisor, Nero.

I gave them my best pitch: 'An activist driving race equality in the heart of government sends out a clear message to Black Britain that change is afoot. Furthermore, through this role we can also champion other marginalised groups left behind, such as Traveller communities and the impoverished white working class too. It would be an advisory role, unpaid for a limited time, two years, and then to be reviewed.'

I did, however, have one condition.

I was aware that if I was given the role, I would be putting my reputation – one I had fought for long and hard – on the line. Most Black people had voted for Corbyn, not May. For me to take on this role, they needed me to demonstrate that they had 'skin in the game', that this was not some empty tick box exercise: 'What does "skin in the game" look like, Simon?'

This was one of those moments when you've got to think quickly, and above all, that you can play at the top table and be taken seriously.

'The way in which the government and the PM can show commitment is by pledging first £20 million, rising to £40 million, to tackle deep systemic race inequality in areas such as education, health and jobs.'

There was silence, but JoJo scribbled some notes and they thanked me and said they'd get back to me soon.

I was called back some weeks later, but this time there were more officials in the room. This was serious. 'The Prime Minister would be honoured for you to chair an advisory group to the world's first Race Disparity Unit.'

Yes, I inwardly yelled.

'Furthermore,' JoJo continued, 'we've thought about your plan for a £40 million fund. As you know, we are also looking at wider disadvantage, so we're going to put in £90 million to tackle the disadvantages that you talk about. And we'll announce it when we announce your role.'

For over twenty years, me and my wonderful team had

moved mountains on sometimes nothing at all and now I'd be seen as part of a £90 million pound force, driving social and racial justice. I could have cried with tears of joy and that overwhelming sensation that now I could get things done, big things. Actually, things were a little more complicated, but for that moment and on launch day, we felt everything was to play for.

Launch day arrived and the media, activists, the Head of the RDU and his team sat in the space usually reserved for Cabinet members, and the Prime Minister launched the RDU with its goal to be transformative. The data would drive policy, the policies would change lives, she said. In a clear demonstration about who she trusted, I was placed on her right-hand side. In my short remarks, I informed the PM that I and the advisory team would be ambitious in our pursuit for greater equality.

So now I had another major job, alongside being CEO at Operation Black Vote: troubleshooting across Whitehall, meeting with ministers, and planning with Nero at No.10. You know you belong, however fleetingly, when you enter the gate to No.10 and the police officers, with their mandatory clipboards, checking who's coming and going, wave me through, with a 'Morning, Simon, all good?'

At this point I want to pay tribute to Nero Ughwujabo, the first Black man to hold this role. He told me very early on that his goal was of course policy driven first and foremost, but equally important was to open the doors to No.10 to Black Britain.

During the time he was there – about two years – more Black people came through those doors than in the previous twenty years.

Few people would turn down an invitation for a meeting or a function at the world's most famous door, No.10 Downing Street. Nero and I realised that he should use the venue a great convening space to hold talks, high-level meetings, or just gatherings where people can believe they belong. We held many meetings for the Race Disparity Unit at No.10. We'd usually meet in the State Dining room, where Nero would preside centre stage: 'Welcome to No.10 Downing Street.' There were many memorable meetings, including the talk about diversity in the film industry from Idris Elba, who was guest speaker with the British Film Institute. But for me, the stand-out meeting was with some of the top people from the world of academia. Oxbridge sent their top teams, Baroness Amos was there representing SOAS at the time, the Office for Students head and many others too. After Nero welcomed everyone, he'd pass over to me to guide the debate, which was the thorny issue of widening participation for Black students along with the lack of Black professors.

Those from the Russell Group universities and Oxbridge seemed particularly nervous. I think they expected me to be a 'David Lammy 2.0' and haul the top universities over the coals for not accepting a single British-born Black student in 2014. But I knew I didn't need to be another Lammy, he'd already laid bare their uncomfortable truths. It was my job to highlight and fast forward the solutions. I began by stating the Race Disparity Unit sessions around education would not be anything akin to the Spanish Inquisition. 'My view,' I informed the assembled group, 'is that we've brought you all here to use your wisdom and insight to find solutions that we all want to see.' I could sense a collective sigh of relief; some, I'm sure, put away their folders with facts and figures to justify the uncomfortable status quo.

It was an excellent meeting. We discussed the value of contextualised offers, which Reading University were leading the charge. Reading were looking not just at A-level grades but taking the time to assess each student's backstory. For example, a disadvantaged student on free school meals or a young carer of a family member who achieves two As and a B could be seen as triple-A student. Their trust in judging through a wider matrix has paid dividends. And most top universities now use more criteria than simply grades to help them assess who has the capability to thrive at the top universities.

In regards to more Black professors, I pushed hard that universities adopted the Race Equality Charter that would give them a framework for change.

I didn't know it at the time, but that meeting and the network of people that came into my orbit was the beginning of my own journey to break a little bit of history, becoming the first Black man to head a Oxbridge college.

* * *

For me, another stand-out moment was the Black History Month event that fashion icon Naomi Campbell attended.

I'd got to know Naomi and her PR guru Alan Edwards about a decade ago when her mother, Valerie Campbell, asked for my assistance. Cadbury's chocolate had just launched a new chocolate bar named Bliss, with the strapline 'Move over, Naomi, there's a new diva in town', with a sprinkling of diamonds – a reference to diamonds that were given to Naomi from disgraced Liberian President Charles Taylor.

'Will you speak to Naomi, Simon,' her mother asked me. 'Everyone tells us you're the guy to fight these slurs that are thrown at our people.'

Most people know Naomi Campbell through a very narrow media prism that highlights her mistakes, which are sometimes very public, but very few care to know about a working-class Black girl who has not only survived but thrived in one of the toughest, meanest, most misogynistic industries on planet Earth: top flight modelling. You can't just be jaw-droppingly good-looking, you've got to be able to fight your corner. More than any other model, Campbell has been at the top of her game for many decades. And the other side that has grown and grown is her fundraising passion for Fashion Aid for Africa. She has raised millions of pounds, and launched the careers of many young Black people. Naomi often tells me, 'Simon, it's my time to give back. Help me do that.'

But this first help was of another nature. The tough woman known to many felt vulnerable to these outside power forces that could rubbish her and sell their chocolate and not even have the decency to make a call. 'Leave it to me, Valerie, I'll get this sorted,' I said, putting down the phone. At first, I had not the slightest idea of how I'd get this chocolate giant to capitulate. I began by calling the head office and speaking to their public relations office. I told them their behaviour was both discourteous and reprehensible, but if they were to take down the ads and issue an apology, the problem would go away. The junior person on the other end of the line promised that someone more senior would call me back, which they did shortly afterwards – only to tell me they would remove nothing because they'd done nothing wrong. I said that if senior management did not see the personal slur and, I threw in for good measure, likening Naomi Campbell to chocolate, then that was on them, but I would call upon the Black community to boycott Cadbury's until they saw sense: 'Do whatever you feel necessary, Mr Woolley. Goodbye.'

So I did just that, I did what was necessary. I called the *Guardian* with our press release: 'I'm calling for a Black boycott of Cadbury's chocolate for their disrespectful behaviour.' They ran the piece. It caught fire and was in most newspapers, both here and abroad. Within twenty-four hours, I got a call for an urgent meeting in Barclay Square.

I arrived there on my own, only to be met by a bank of lawyers and senior people flown in from Geneva to get rid of this problem.

'This meeting doesn't have to be long,' I suggested, 'we

just have to be clear. The poster comes down, you apologise, we're done. If not …'

'No, no, Mr Woolley, we think that's fine. It shouldn't have happened and we'll be having a strong word with our ad agency about this.'

After the apology, a statement was thrashed out and the campaign cut short. I challenged them to work with us and the ad agency, which was probably all white, to begin a conversation about race and diversity within the industry. 'Yes, yes, yes, let's do that, Simon,' they said while handing me a goodie bag of all their chocolate brands.

I'd got what Naomi wanted and she was over the moon, but I could probably have got more from Cadbury's, maybe a donation to Naomi's charity or something. But this was never a 'shake down', it was simply a campaign for decency and justice.

So fast forward a decade, and I had the thought to call Naomi through Alan Edwards and ask her to fly over for an event we had organised at No.10 for Black History Month and to meet with Prime Minister Theresa May: 'I'd only do this for Simon,' she insisted he inform me.

Her trip had about a forty-eight-hour turnaround and her scheduling was tight. To make matters worse, the whole event was in jeopardy because the day's Brexit discussions with twenty-seven heads of state was running over time, and Naomi had her flight back home booked so she could get back to work.

I was on my way to Downing Street when I got a call:

'Simon, we have a problem. The PM is going to be an hour late and Naomi has to leave soon or she'll miss her flight.'

I walked into No.10 and everyone was in a bit of a panic – Naomi's people, the PM's people. Everyone had worked so hard for the event to make it special.

'Right, let's see how we fix this. Flight time, bags done, route known. Once we've got that we can make a judgement as to when Naomi has to leave. We can do this.' And we did. Naomi couldn't stay for long but she and the PM discussed how they might assist young African girls in poverty to get better educated. 'Simon, you're wonderful, you make everything seem simple,' Naomi said, before being whisked off back to New York. To be honest, I kept thinking, *I'm going to let them both down at this rate*, not that I let them know it.

My evening hadn't finished. We had two hundred guests next door waiting for the PM and Nero had just informed me that the PM wanted me to introduce her, in five minutes.

Leave it to me. All good.

I got up on to the small platform and stood at the lectern. 'Ladies and gentlemen, brothers and sisters, for the next two hours, *mi casa es tu casa*.' Roars of laughter. 'I haven't told the Prime Minister yet, but it's same time next week too. When the PM comes, I want you to give her a big round of applause – I promise you, she's not going to dance.' I could see even the Prime Minister laughing at that one.

We had a great evening, relaxed but with that prevailing message: we belong, this is ours too.

I was later told by a senior aide that that evening was one of the contributing factors that led the PM to elevate me to the House of Lords. 'People trust him,' she said, 'and this will empower him to do more.'

* * *

Sometimes you are on the up and feel you are making progress and at others the situation changes and you feel like you are going backwards. It can be immensely frustrating but I have learned, to an extent, that you have to ride the ebb and flow. There will always be disappointments.

For example, when we sadly lost the wonderful, inspiring Bernie Grant in 2000. Bernie was one of the very first Black MPs to be elected, in 1987, along with Diane Abbott and Paul Boateng. He was a politician not just for the people of Tottenham but for Black people, globally. In his office he had a team of about eight people because almost every Black person, wherever they lived, would see him as their MP regardless of who their actual MP was. Letters would come into Bernie's office and he would answer them all. Bernie was bitterly disappointed that the Blair government had never given him a key role, despite all the skills and expertise that he had. But Blair's government was about micromanaging everything and Bernie was not to be managed, he sought to be respected. But it broke his heart that he couldn't use his life experiences at the highest level.

David Lammy replaced Bernie as MP for Tottenham. He was, is, extremely bright and was elevated very quickly within the Labour Party. He landed a few junior ministerial roles but many felt he could have been a bigger advocate for race equality. I think he would perhaps say now that he could have spoken out more but I have to concede that I for one didn't fully understand party politics then, particularly when you get to that ministerial level. You have to toe the line and unless you're one of the big beasts, you get told what to do. It is easy to be idealistic about what someone can achieve when you get a seat at that table, and disappointing when you perceive that someone isn't using their platform. Even if, realistically, they would have little leverage at that early stage of their career.

For many Black politicians there is this huge added responsibility. Of course, you're elected to represent your constituency, but then there's the expectation from your own racial or religious community, and the wider Black, Asian and minority ethnic communities is enormous.

And just to add to that impossible mix: our own communities are our feistiest critics.

For example, if I do a radio or TV interview then one or two people will say well done; if it's poor, a Black chorus will tell you exactly what you could have done better. This isn't even mentioning your normal racist detractors. At times, it's a heavy burden. You're also acutely aware there's rarely a second chance if you fall short and make an error. For many Black people, it's one strike and you're out.

Take Boris Johnson, for instance. He's made more big mistakes any other living politician today and yet, like others before him – and you can name many more of them – he gets a second, third, fourth chance. He can brush it off, reinvent himself, and away he goes again.

Boris Johnson and his team ran a brilliantly poisoned campaign in the 2008 mayoral election. They knew they couldn't really go after Ken Livingstone, despite Livingstone making some of his own damning comments, such as the 'concentration camp' remarks to the Jewish reporter. But Johnson had Andrew Gilligan and Veronica Wadley, who was editor of the *Evening Standard* and is now Baroness Fleet and chairman of the Arts Council, on his side and was able to use the *Evening Standard* as his mouthpiece. So who did he go after? Lee Jasper. The press went full steam ahead to discredit Jasper and anybody associated with him and Livingstone. It was nasty. They also went for Doreen Lawrence because of the funding she had got from Ken Livingstone. In fact, all those Black groups that were being funded by Livingstone and Jasper were on Andrew Gilligan's hit list.

The police froze Jasper's bank accounts so he couldn't touch any money while they investigated the allegations. But nothing was found because nothing was there. I got a call from Gilligan, who told me they'd investigated me and investigated Operation Black Vote and the reason why we hadn't been more of a target was because we never took any offers of money but he wanted to warn me that we were on their radar and would get me if needs be. It was chilling – it really demonstrated the incestuous nexus between politics and the media: a kind of clubby, mutual back scratching.

The Black community in London, particularly any organisation that had received funding from Ken Livingstone's administration, felt like we were under siege from the *Evening Standard*. Most people headed for the hills because they thought, '*How can we stand up against the* Evening Standard?' It's so hard to challenge accusations made in the media, particularly when you're a small organisation with no money. Nobody's going to believe you. But I kept my head up. I wrote a piece in the *Guardian* simply arguing that Lee Jasper was a good man. I went on a BBC London show presented by Geoff Schumann and went head-to-head with Andrew Gilligan. It was the right thing to do but it was not pleasant. I assume my phones are tapped; I assume that people have been digging around for dirt for years; I assume that there are entities that would seek to destroy me and that is worrying.

So I do feel we are held to much higher standards than white people in similar positions. And at the same time, while I am very proud of the progress we have made and of all those who have worked to make that happen, there are still too few of us in public office and positions of leadership so we are in a sense more visible and, I believe, under much more scrutiny than our white counterparts.

It is of course not just in politics where the penalties are far harsher if you are not white. There are many examples I could give but former Wimbledon midfielder Robbie Earle is a case in point. In June 2010, he had his £150,000-a-year

ITV contract cancelled after giving away some World Cup tickets, which were later used by a Dutch marketing company for a stunt without his knowledge. He was a great footballer and is still a great pundit as he now works in the States. In sharp contrast, ex-Liverpool player Jamie Carragher spat on a fourteen-year-old girl and was suspended for six months, before going back on TV like nothing had happened. Can you imagine a Black player ever being seen on TV again if he had spat in a girl's face? Never in a million years. Yet Robbie Earle, who gave out some tickets to a match that he was allowed to apply for was dumped, never to be seen on British TV again.

* * *

There's a theory in social psychology called 'system justification', which refers to defending or justifying the status quo even when it clearly disadvantages them. On a simple level, I guess we've all done it to a certain extent. It can feel much less uncomfortable or challenging to keep the blinkers on in regards to the systemic racism or the microaggression may be experienced on a regular basis. The temptation to say to yourself, 'Everything's fine! That wasn't racist,' is understandable because it avoids getting weighed down by having to confront these things consciously all the time. At its extreme, however, it can a bit of a psychosis in which your default is to deny it altogether, or to say, 'Yes, but it's never happened to me ...'

I understand why people take that trajectory. What I

cannot accept is that Black, Asian and minority ethnic people in positions of power, positions of authority, take this stance. In people's individual daily lives that might be their survival mechanism, but when you are making decisions and influencing policy that will impact millions of other people's lives, your denial then becomes very problematic. When you've got the information, the evidence in front of your eyes and you are still blinkered, then that must be a case of wilful denial.

CHAPTER 8

FATHERHOOD

I didn't want this memoir to be a deep dive into my private life. By definition, that's private. But then again, since I've become a father, it's made me really think about what I do, why I do it, and what sort of legacy I want to leave for my son. It's been the driving force behind what I do for the past fifteen years.

At the age of forty-four, I thought that becoming a father wasn't going to happen, even though for many years I hankered after that. A long-term relationship had just come to a natural end. I felt sad at the prospect of not being a father, which is stupid really because us men potentially still have a greater option in these matters. But I was beginning to accept that if I dated women of a similar age to me, it could be too late. It did cross my mind that I could follow my mum and dad and foster or adopt. But I was getting ahead of myself – I was single, after all!

Facing the end of our long-term relationship – over ten years – sadly but amicably, my ex-partner and I began the process of untangling the threads of our lives. I remained in London and she returned to Spain, but we stayed in touch and visited each other. And then, to both of our wonderful surprise, we discovered that we were going to be parents.

We could hardly believe it, we thought this was a sign that we were meant to be together. I knew then that I was meant to be a father.

* * *

I grew up with two loving parents, although I lost them both relatively young, but I suppose the fact that I was adopted and never knew my biological father may have affected my desire to be a father myself. More than that – to endeavour to be the best father I could be. Who knows? I'm sure I'd get a myriad of responses from the psychiatrist's chair why that might be if I ever put the question to them. What I do know is that I had a gut feeling that being a dad would be the most wonderful thing I could do.

My adopted father, Dan Fox, had a big influence on me, not so much as an emotional role model, but as a dad who provides and protects. Like many men born in the early part of the twentieth century, he wasn't an outwardly emotional man. He went to work and I went to school. He'd come home, watch a bit of TV and then go to his room. There was a pattern and a lovely familiarity to our home. My dad was a good man, and although he was born in an era when fathers took the belt to 'discipline' their children, he never so lifted a finger to me or my brother. But one of my life's biggest regrets is that he didn't live long enough that I reached an age where I could sit down with him and have a conversation about life, politics or anything deep. So, much as I loved and admired my dad, I knew that I would never want that emotional distance with my own child.

My dad was a real homebody and didn't spend much time out. My mother would take us to visit her sisters in Wales in the school holidays but Dan never came, he would stay behind and work. Except for one time, when he did show up. My uncle brought him up and he just showed up out of the blue. That was probably one of the funniest and most magical moments of my childhood when he suddenly appeared at my aunt's. It was so special and unexpected that he was there and the whole house lit up.

One thing I definitely did learn from Dan was how to work hard. He was a man with a great work ethic. He saw his role as a provider and he was our protector too. I fondly remember as a young child watching my dad come home from work; a big-set man, with his slow gait, suit on, shoes polished. I've told you about how he would reach into his pocket to give us a Bar Six each. It was his way of showing us he was thinking of us, I suppose.

When I think about him now, the image that so often comes to mind is of that photo taken of us when I had first come to live with him and my mum – Pippi – my face filled with uncertainty, his big arms around me an unspoken promise to keep me safe.

When he suddenly passed away in 1974, it did hit me very hard. It was desperate, too, to see my strong mum crying. So, I wanted to be there for her too. Fact is that I was already starting to learn at that age – like so many kids from my sort of background – how to be self-sufficient and resilient. That ultimately, the person I could most depend on would be myself. I think that's why my dad's death, far from derailing me as it might have done, probably made me stronger.

* * *

One day during the pregnancy Luca's mum said to me, 'Would you tell me the truth? Would you like to have a boy or a girl?'

Well, I wasn't sure what to say. I really didn't want to say the wrong thing. In my head, I knew that it didn't make any difference to how much I would love my child, but in my heart, I knew I did have a preference. But I played it safe and truthfully said, 'We're going to have a prince or princess!'

And then she said, 'I went to the doctor's for a check-up and he said, "You know it's a boy?"' Typically Spanish! And she'd said, 'Well, I do now!'

I cried; I physically wept tears of joy. I'd have been thrilled with a daughter, I know I would, but the idea of having a son thrilled me with all the potential things we might do.

Not that I couldn't do the same things with a daughter, but I was still to some extent a product of my upbringing that had certain ideas of what boys and girls do. The most incredible and almost overwhelming feeling was that I was going to be a father: it was definitely happening.

When Luca was born, he came out screaming. He also came out with a head like an alien. Lots of babies are born with a bit of a conehead and it tends to resolve itself within days or even hours of the birth. It's nothing to worry about. Of course, I didn't know this at the time and just thought, *Oh my God, my son's an alien.* A screaming, pointy-headed alien. But I didn't care. It didn't matter; he was my son. Then the nurse gave him to me and I put him against my chest as the three of us were cuddled up together and he stopped crying. And that was it. The most wondrous moment of my entire life. (OK, between you and me, maybe the second-most. The first was when my son was playing a local football team and he took on four players, or was it five? He nutmegged the last player, stepped round them and chipped the ball over the goalkeeper's head, then turned to look for me as if to say: 'See that, Dad? That one's for you.')

Luca was born in the Central Hospital in Baracaldo, Bilbao. His grandfather had said to me, slightly dramatically, 'Simon, I just want to ask you one favour . . . Do you mind if the baby is born in Bilbao rather than London?'

I had thought Waltham Forest Hospital would have been good enough to do the job but I had no problem with that plan, though I did ask the reason.

'Well, above all, if the boy is born in Bilbao, and if he is a good footballer, it means he can play for Athletic Bilbao!'

Which is true. You can only play for this team if you are born in the Basque Country or learned your skills at a Basque club. It's the only team in the modern footballing world playing at a high level to have a policy like this. If you were not born in the Basque Country, you can play for any other team in the world but not Athletic Bilbao. So that was the deal I made with my son's grandfather.

Fast forward thirteen years and Luca did get a trial for Athletic Bilbao, which was one of the proudest days for his grandfather, and for me. Watching his first grandson run out on the training field in the Athletic Bilbao kit he had bought him was very special for Luca's grandfather, who comes from a region where football is a religion. It was a dream come true for him. From a very young age, Luca was very sports-minded and loved football, although so many football coaches coached the love out of the game for him with their screaming and shouting whenever a mistake was made. So professional football was not going to be for him and, in all honesty, I'm not sorry. A lot of very talented kids go into the football academies at a young age and then that is their life. They may work their hardest and get tantalisingly close but, ten years later, be left with little or, worse, nothing. In most other professions you would be set for life after ten years plus of dedicated hard work.

As he grew from a baby to a toddler to a fun, happy child, I watched his every move. I knew the kid's heartbeat.

I knew when he was down, or anxious and of course when he was bursting with joy. There were all the milestones, clichés, perhaps, of seeing him take his first steps, ride a bike for the first time. And the bumps in the road that parents everywhere will recognise. The dread of anything happening to them – does that ever lessen? – the almost overwhelming desire to take their pain away, to suffer it for them, when they are hurt or sad.

I think my instinct was right – I was meant to be a father. And although it didn't go according to plan with his mum and me, we worked out how to be the best parents and very close friends.

When the country went into lockdown in 2020, the three of us lived together. It really was a time of great uncertainty and emotional on many levels. It made us all think about what was important to us. This was doubly so for me, particularly watching, as we all did, so many Black and Asian people who were among those dying at a shockingly disproportionate rate. Remember, of the first one hundred doctors and medical staff that died, ninety-eight were Black or Asian.

While it was difficult to find silver linings during that period, getting to spend that precious time with my teenage son, now taller and very much stronger than me but nonetheless affectionate, was incredibly special. That moment will never happen again, right? It's true to say that 24/7 lockdown brought us closer as a family.

* * *

One of the most fascinating – and sometimes scary – parts of parenting is seeing your child become their own fully-fledged, increasingly independent of you, person. As many of you know that independence doesn't extend to lifts to the station, washing and ironing clothes, and money for takeaways. Actually, with money in general, that's not been a big issue. Luca, in the last few years wanted to earn his own money; first buying and selling brand-new training shoes, and more recently, NFTs. And before you ask me 'What's an NFT?', I'm going to put my hands up and say, 'I don't know.' His explanation, which sounds real, but slightly scary and bonkers, is that you buy virtual art – not the sort you hang on your wall – and then you punt if someone will pay more for it, which then increases the value, until someone isn't willing to pay for it. Then you're stuffed, because the art, that you could never put on your wall, is now worthless. We all got that, twenty-first-century capitalism? Me neither!

But I'm not going lie, I have a sneaking admiration for his 'side hustles', along with bots and other tricks that he thinks will give him an edge. I did it with the football and theatre tickets, his currency is training shoes and NFTs. But beyond that, I like that fact that one of the things that Luca has either inherited or learnt from me is how to be a fighter, to stand up for what he believes in. For example, when he was about eleven, some of his friends who were Black, were being homophobic. He said to them, 'Hang on a second. We all rage when we have racism, right? What you're doing is the same because someone's gay.' When he told me I couldn't be prouder. I thought, *job nearly done*!

I also think he's surpassed me in some ways. When I was his age I desperately wanted to be liked, and I still do to an extent, although it's only a very small group of people where that matters. I think he's more sure of himself than I was at his age and no longer needs group approval. I remember him saying once about a supposedly 'cool' group at school, 'Dad, I can't be with that lot, you should hear the rubbish they talk about.' If the group dynamic is mean, he won't fit in with it.

As parents we try to give our children self-assurance and resilience for the things they will undoubtedly have to face in their lives, to cope with a sometimes cruel world. Luca's journey will undoubtedly be different to mine – he has a cushion of privilege that cannot be ignored. I'm sure that his hustler spirit and standing up for what he believes in will undoubtedly help, particularly in a world that is only just, really and truthfully, coming to terms what systemic race inequality really is and what it means.

On a number of occasions, and to my horror, my son, who is proud of his mixed heritage, has to learn to deal with the type of in-your-face racism that I thought had been consigned to the 1970s. It might – arguably – not be a prevalent on the streets, and instead has moved online, and has become ever more virulent. Be aware that as your children play Fortnight and other games across the country and beyond, brutal, gutter racism is alive and kicking.

The trick is to teach him to deal with the hatred, but to avoid hating the race of the people spewing their vitriolic hatred at him – white people, in other words. Given that the person he loves most in the world – his mother – is white, this can be an emotional challenge that as a family we confront together.

He first started to come across the more subtle yet no less debilitating form of racism in his early teens. He would go to Westfield shopping centre with his friends, and if the group happened to be mainly Black, they'd notice they were being followed around by the security guards. Or when he was at school and the dinner lady told them off for messing about. She said, 'Why are you behaving like animals? Why can't you behave like them?' and then pointed to the white kids. Learning their own resilience mechanisms, one of Luca's black friends responded, 'Ma'am, what animal are you referring to?' and then mimicked a chanting monkey.

In earlier years it was challenging but a lot easier. I recall sitting in a restaurant, Luca must have been about three or four, as inquisitive as hell. And he turned and said, 'Dad, see that man over there? He's Black, and you're brown, then what colour am I?' As quick as a flash, as if I somehow knew I would have to confront this question sooner or later, I said, 'Caramel gold, son. Special chosen.' He looked at me, smiled and went back to his food.

Before Luca, I'd spent ten years driving Operation Black Vote, fighting for social and racial justice. Now it had so much more meaning. I was literally fighting for a better world for my son. My energy levels ramped up; forget turbo charge, or catalytic converter, I was in mission-led, rocket mode.

* * *

The other upside of having Luca – there's more? – is that he definitely helped to strengthen the relationship I have with Lolita, my birth mother. She wanted to know him and I thought it was important that he knows her. I have told my son I have two mothers. One white, one black, a little bit complicated in between, but it's worked out fine, very fine. 'Without them,' I say to him, 'there'd be no you.'

And they get on great, as he does with his beloved grandparents in Spain.

I hope that my own experiences have made me a good dad. When things got tough for me and his mum we did everything to make sure that nothing much changed for him. I never knew my blood father, and barely knew my adopted father, Dan. But I really know my son, and he really knows me. I suspect you envisaged me smiling when I wrote that last line. Correct.

CHAPTER 9

THIS IS MODERN BRITAIN

L et's go back to the 2015 election, which would not only change the world as we knew it, it would also have a huge impact on my life personally.

After five years of Conservative/Liberal Democrat coalition, David Cameron and his team were desperate to ensure that this time they won enough seats to govern alone. They concluded that they would have to reach out to the right of the electorate they feared was being lured away from them by UKIP Leader Nigel Farage and his cohorts – some of whom Cameron had previously dismissed as 'fruitcakes', 'loonies' and 'closet racists'. To do this, and to deal with some of the grumbling from his own Eurosceptic back-benchers, he promised a referendum on Britain's membership of the European Union. Back then, the idea that Britain would leave the EU was not only not on most people's minds, but to the mainstream seemed fanciful, preposterous, even. The average person didn't give a hoot about whether we should be in or not, they just enjoyed the benefits of being in the EU without knowing it – the Erasmus education exchange programme, the freedom to travel and to work wherever we wanted – so I guess David Cameron and George Osborne thought it was a free bet – *We'll give them a referendum, easily win it and it'll be business as usual. The question will be answered and we'll be back on track.*

Very early on, I became worried about the trajectory that the Brexit debate was taking. It was clear that it was bringing into sharp and ugly focus something that had been simmering for a long time. The coalition government had been under pressure to bring down the numbers of people coming into the UK, with the *Daily Mail* and the other right-wing newspapers going after the immigration issue day after day. It didn't matter that all the data showed that migrants from Europe provided a net gain to the UK economy – that on the whole we benefited from their entrepreneurialism, expertise and energy, and that they would do some jobs that Britons are reluctant to do – fruit picking, for example.

The events of 9/11 and particularly 7/7 changed British politics in a number of ways. The UK government had to be seen to be confronting the threat of homegrown terrorism. Appalled as anyone by the attacks, the Muslim community was isolated as Hindus and Sikhs sought to set themselves apart to avoid being the target of the burgeoning Islamophobia from those who saw all Asian people as the same. As the Brexit debate gathered pace and vitriol, Muslims became a particular target of the right-wing press and the anti-immigrant narrative they constructed. It had little to do with our membership of the EU, but it would have a wide and lasting impact.

It was an easy sell for Farage and those of his ilk. After six years of austerity, which had impacted impoverished communities across the country, decimating public services, it suited them enormously to tell poor white people that everything that was wrong was down to 'Brussels' and 'the immigrants'. The narrative of Brexit positioned immigrants against white Britons, telling British people, 'You're poor because of *them*.' This served to break open the cracks that were appearing in our society into great divisions – and we are still dealing with the fallout.

If you're struggling, I understand that you might want someone to blame. I absolutely don't think that all Brexiteers are racist – but I'm pretty sure that the vast majority of racists are Brexiteers. The other reality about Brexit, of course, is that it showed that there is a significant number of people in the UK who are deeply racist. How many? Who knows. I do know the situation here is anywhere near as bad as it is in other European countries. We've had an anti-racist conversation and anti-racist movement for fifty or sixty years now, which makes us the best place in Europe when it comes to race equality. But to argue that there is no longer a problem with racists is to be in denial of reality. And this is what Brexit horribly exposed, and what some who drove Brexit nurtured.

* * *

What will, I think, be remembered and analysed into the future, is the amount of misinformation that was peddled in the run-up to the referendum, stoking xenophobia and racism. For example, in April 2016, the *Express* led with the headline, 'EU loophole could see 77 MILLION Turks head to Britain, warn Farage and Johnson'. Which was of course entirely impossible, as not only was Turkey not a member of the EU, the chance of it becoming one was looking slim, and even if it did, that would mean the entire population of Turkey decamping to the UK.

At Operation Black Vote, we were increasingly concerned by the toxic climate such narratives were fostering. As ever, we remained non-partisan in our campaigning, focusing on mobilising as many people from Black, Asian and ethnic minority communities to register to vote and to engage in the EU referendum debate. As we had for every general election, we began working on a poster campaign with our media partners Saatchi & Saatchi to highlight just how vital political participation was at this time.

I had first met the advertising magnate Magnus Djaba sometime around early 2015. I had gone to a roundtable discussion in some swanky restaurant, where I had been seated next to this sharp-suited Black man, with whom I'd had a very interesting discussion about Black politics, though I didn't really know who he was.

As I was about to leave, he said to me, 'Simon, I really like what you have to say, I really like what you're about. And I work for an organisation that might be able to help.' With that, he handed me his card. But I must have been very tired because I didn't look at it – I put it straight in my pocket and headed home. Later, I dug into my inside jacket pocket and pulled out the card: 'Magnus Djaba, Global President, Saatchi & Saatchi and CEO, Saatchi & Saatchi UK'. I had to examine my own internalised prejudices at that point. Throughout our free-ranging and warm conversation, shamefully it hadn't occurred to me that he could be in charge of this big international company – the only Black CEO of a major advertising agency, in fact.

Not long afterwards, I contacted Magnus and visited his offices, where we had an incredible meeting. Magnus explained that not only was he interested in working with Operation Black Vote, he wanted to do so as if we were a high-paying client – 'throwing the kitchen sink at the project' was the way he described it. He envisaged putting together a campaign that was bold and brave – this meant a strong, impactful message that would work hard to deliver our objectives, while showcasing his company as a creative agency, hopefully winning awards and therefore more business. I just couldn't believe my ears: the work he was proposing to do for us pro bono costs the big brands many millions of pounds.

Two or three months later, before the 2015 general election, Magnus called me back in. The storyboard his team had put together was based on the fact that our institutions are predominantly white, one colour, and not diverse or colourful. But if Black people voted, then we'd have a different story. Our institutions would be inclusive, the delivery would be representative, it would be a game changer. Their idea was to start a conversation by painting Black people's faces white. I thought about it for a second and said, 'I love it. It's brilliant.'

They told me afterwards that they didn't expect me to go with the idea. For white people to do blackface is offensive and rooted in racism so if we showed Black people painting themselves white to have a conversation about monolithic institutions, would we be accused of hypocrisy? It was highly likely but I was prepared to take the flak for what I could see would be a powerful and eye-catching campaign, so I gave the green light.

We knew we would need some big stars involved to pull this off. I'd known the footballer Sol Campbell for years and so we got in touch with him. He's a bit of a political animal himself, even, in February 2015 announcing his intention to stand for London Mayor, although in the end he wasn't shortlisted. He agreed to the ad campaign, and his involvement led to a discussion with the Hollywood actor David Harewood. Then the rap artist Tinie Tempah came on board, which was a huge story. We also reached out to the BBC presenter and wheelchair basketball player

Ade Adepitan, who agreed to get involved. I have to say, they absolutely put their necks on the line for Operation Black Vote. For a Black man to paint his face white was extremely brave. It was a bold campaign and we didn't know how it would be received. The icing on the cake was that Magnus had convinced the legendary photographer Rankin to shoot a short film and the accompanying posters. Not coming from the world of glitz and glamour I had no idea who Rankin was, but when I met him, he said, 'Hey man, I like your work, and my wife does too.' He gave me a hug. 'Let's do this.'

The message was that if we didn't engage, if we didn't register to vote, then we were taking the colour out of Britain. Our institutions would remain as white as they had always been. And of course, it went crazy. Every newspaper, every TV station covered the story. It gave me the platform to talk about why we did it.

I spoke with David Harewood shortly after the campaign: 'Simon, man, what have you done to me? I've never done anything like it. I've taken a lot of flak, a lot of abuse. But there's been so much love for me from Black people.' He said that he had up until this point always been judged as an actor, for his skill in the role he was playing, but now, 'I'm being judged for who I am and not what I'm doing.'

We've been friends ever since. David went on to make several programmes on politics, including the wonderful *Will Britain Ever Have a Black Prime Minister?* for BBC Two (2016). I think politics was probably always in his DNA but

I like to think that the campaign in 2015 helped him into a position from which he could speak out.

So, skip forward a year, to the increasingly toxic debate around Brexit, and we sat down again with Saatchi & Saatchi to talk about another campaign. I said, 'Look, it's a small minority but there is a very, very racist vote out there. We know these people will vote. And so Black people, if nothing else, must counter that.' If we didn't, it would be handing influence to these people and the momentum behind that 'little England' xenophobia might grow.

As usual, Saatchi & Saatchi threw their best minds at the project. We sat around the table in their offices and they showed me some slides outlining the concept. Larissa Vince was my point person at Saatchi at the time. She is mixed heritage, her mum is Caribbean, and she is now CEO of the ad agency TBWA. So now we have two ad agency CEOs with African-Caribbean heritage. What I always really admired about Saatchi & Saatchi is the way they pushed the envelope and came up with challenging ideas to force people to stop and think.

In this way, they were fantastic partners but this particular concept pushed me to the limit of my comfort zone. What they showed me was a seesaw. On one side was an Asian woman with a nice demeanour; on the other side, they had a skinhead wearing bovver boots, snarling with a raised fist. There was no indication of which way either person was voting, it was designed to show that each vote carried the same weight: 'A vote is a vote'.

I said that I liked the idea but I couldn't accept the fist. The fist denoted aggression, violence, whereas I wanted to characterise this as the politics of xenophobia and not far-right supremacy so they changed the fist into a pointing finger and I said we were good to go.

The day we launched, I was due to go to Wales to a voter registration event. As soon as Saatchi & Saatchi put it out there, we were gaining plenty of interest from the get-go. But then Nigel Farage spotted the campaign and dramatically, and to some extent successfully, flipped the concept, accusing us of going 'down a route of sectarian politics', saying, ironically, that we were 'trying to divide society'. Just a few weeks later, it should be remembered, Farage would put out his infamous 'Breaking Point' billboard, using a picture of what were in fact non-white migrants and refugees fleeing a war zone, with the line: 'We must break free of the EU and take back control of our borders'. Two hours after the unveiling, the Labour MP Jo Cox was murdered by far-right extremist, Thomas Mair. It was the most appalling, gut-wrenching, sickening political ad that I've seen in recent years and rightly caused outrage. Nevertheless, Farage had the gall to tell a reporter, 'I know Simon Woolley, I respect him, but he is essentially calling Brexit voters racist. And that makes him a racist.'

Well, with that, Farage unleashed the dogs of hell on me and Operation Black Vote.

During the Brexit referendum campaign, Operation Black Vote was thrown into the biggest crisis of its existence.

We had always faced one challenge or another, mainly with regards to funding. At our peak, we had been able to employ twelve staff, but after austerity, we were threadbare again, down to just six. And here we were, facing an onslaught from the media, with very few hands available to get on deck.

Looking back, I now understand how so many elements came together to create the perfect storm. Thanks to Brexit, never in recent political history had the climate been so toxic: it was vicious and the main players – politicians and the Brexit lobby in the media – were taking no prisoners. A race to the bottom, it was downright nasty. Maybe we were a little naïve to think that we could cut through that toxicity. What I hadn't realised was how important it is that you have the mechanism to control the narrative. Once you lose the narrative, you're on the backfoot.

Farage had said that our campaign was racist. Many newspapers questioned the ad, asking, 'Is this a racist ad?' Simon Woolley – you're a racist. Discuss.' Once things started to unfold, I went on BBC News along with someone from UKIP. I said that we would take no lessons, no lectures from the most xenophobic party in modern history. When I looked at social media afterwards, it seemed our message was cutting through – people were saying, 'Well done, you put him aside easily.' But the next morning, I was travelling from North Wales to Cardiff for another event when I got a call from the comms person at Saatchi & Saatchi.

'Simon, we have got a shit show,' she said. 'All the channels want to speak to you. Are you OK with this?'

'This is what we're here for,' I said. 'Let's face this down and win the argument.'

So, that morning, for about two hours, I was on practically every single news, current affairs or chat show radio programme in the UK. And the assault on me was vicious. Indeed, Vanessa Feltz of BBC London went for the jugular and called me a racist.

I replied, 'Vanessa, I'm highlighting that this election, this referendum, is so toxic with its xenophobia that all we've done is call it out, call out the blatantly obvious.'

But she was having none of it: 'No, you're the racist because you're insinuating that all Brexiters are racist.'

Of course, we never said that. And the poster did not say which way each person was voting – the media jumped to that conclusion all by themselves.

'What I was doing was demonstrating a caricature of a racist,' I replied. 'Now, if you're telling me that all Brexiters look like the man in our poster, then you're sorely mistaken. We used an outlandish caricature to demonstrate it was the thug that we were targeting, not normal British voters.'

But the media were out for blood. Sure enough, there soon appeared a two-page spread by none other than the *Daily Mail*'s Katie Hopkins, the xenophobic, Islamophobic, populist shit-stirrer of division, under the extraordinarily long headline: 'It's bad enough spending tax-payers' money to encourage black people to vote but telling them HOW to vote is outrageous'.

Then the *Daily Mail* published a piece questioning our funding and our status as a charity. Of course, the Charity Commission said they'd investigate, so that the following day, the *Mail* was able to run with: 'Charity probe into "racist" poster: Fury as it emerges Cabinet Office gave money to body behind controversial advert'. We could see that they were determined to take us down by any means necessary.

The UK government said that we had to clearly demonstrate that no government money that we had received to promote voter registration was used for this ad. And I could say no, it wasn't, because it was pro bono: this was all Operation Black Vote. So, everybody was heading for cover and there were journalists outside my house.

We had an emergency board meeting. For the first time ever in our history, they were angry with me. They asked, 'OK, so what are we going to do?' I said that we needed to go out on the front foot, rather than hunker down and hope it blows over. And I remembered that Saatchi & Saatchi had had another campaign idea. The board wanted me to keep my head down but I argued that it would make us seem guilty. I don't know how we did it, but we convinced them that we should be proud of who we are and release the next ad.

The next poster recreated that infamous picture of David Cameron and Boris Johnson with the Bullingdon

Club at Oxford, standing in their morning suits, looking like they knew they were born to rule. In the photo that Saatchi & Saatchi created, the privileged, young white men were replaced with British people from African, Asian and Caribbean communities. It looked fantastic. The strapline was, 'Deciding Britain's future is everyone's birthright'.

We put it out in the media and many outlets ran with the poster. I gave a quote, explaining our rationale: 'We felt it important to speak out because this referendum and its debate will shape the nation's future for a generation. It should not be driven by the few, and certainly should not be decided by a minority of small, interested parties, even privileged parties. We felt the juxtaposition of the infamous image replaced by a snapshot of the UK's minority communities in so many ways couldn't be more stark: the powerful versus the powerless, the constantly heard against the voiceless.'

We were back on track and back on the airwaves, talking about how politics could be more inclusive, but it had been an incredibly bruising encounter with the right-wing media that had put Operation Black Vote into crisis and demonstrated just how much vitriol and loathing was now present in the media and infusing the Brexit debate.

* * *

Like many of us, right up to election night, I didn't believe that Vote Leave, factions of which campaign had relied on misinformation and more xenophobia than I had dreamed was present in modern Britain, would win. There were so many reasons for this that will probably still be being pulled apart in years to come as the ramifications of that night continue to play out.

It didn't help of course that Labour leader Jeremy Corbyn, who was no great defender of the European Union, largely stayed out of the debate. His socialistic instincts were that it was another power club that didn't have working-class people's best interests at heart. I also think he may have calculated that he could stand back and let the Tories hack each other to political death.

On the morning of 24 June 2016, when the result was confirmed, I felt like I'd suffered a bereavement. There's no other way to describe it. I felt utterly bereft and saddened to my heart. I might have cried. Not least because my son was born in Spain and has British and Spanish passports. It took me a long time to get over Brexit. I lost or nearly lost many friends over it. I struggled to understand when friends – Black, white, Jewish – voted Brexit because I'd seen all the xenophobia and simply thought that we didn't have the luxury to say we don't like the French interfering with our politics when, in many ways, the EU's human rights-centred politics would help push back on this. Not everything about the EU is ideal, it certainly has some major flaws, but was this really the path we had chosen to go down instead?

That wave of xenophobia, for at least another year, seemed to be off the leash. I went on the James O'Brien show on LBC about three or four days after the election.

The interview was in the news afterwards due to a call James took from a German lady who was living somewhere outside London.

'I haven't been out of my house for a week, since the election, because I'm frightened,' she said, audibly distressed. 'I have lived here for the past thirty years, with my husband, who's a doctor, and we've been part of the community. My husband recently died, but I've had neighbours telling me, "We've won Brexit, now go home." I've even had excrement put through my door.' She then started to cry. It was the most heart-breaking call that I've ever known on the radio and to be in the studio listening to that was awful.

Of course, with xenophobia and racism there has historically been a hierarchy of dislike that extends to hate, which can be fluid too. At the top of the tree in this country are Muslims, Roma, Irish travellers then African Caribbeans. The Jewish community, Chinese and Eastern Europeans. But Western Europeans generally got a pass. But now white, Western Europeans with Christian heritage were being reminded for the first time that they were foreigners here too. How had we come to this point, in twenty-first-century Britain? This was the post-Brexit climate.

And of course, it cannot be forgotten that at the same time, on the other side of the Atlantic, the political climate was becoming increasingly poisonous as we headed towards the American election in the November of that year. Initially, it was unthinkable that Donald Trump would win. He was a clown, a reality TV shill, a media joke. Even his own people said he really didn't give himself a chance and yet they saw a glimmer of hope in what happened with Brexit. In this country, we looked on as similar anti-immigrant sentiment was expounded from podiums, people were scapegoated and economic realities manipulated to ultimately bring an ignorant racist and xenophobe to power.

David Cameron inevitably fell on his sword and resigned on 24 June 2016. The Conservative Party began tearing themselves apart. The leadership contest was supposed to be between Michael Gove and Boris Johnson, but then these two blustering alpha males ended up effectively politically destroying other, paving the way for Theresa May to be crowned without opposition. These were some of the darkest times I had known in my life as an activist; I had no idea that May becoming prime minister would go on to be a life changer and create more opportunities for me and aspects of my work than I could have thought possible.

* * *

It's fair to say that, after it was announced that I was on the advisory team of the Race Disparity Unit, my life had changed dramatically. Not just in that space, where, for, the previous twenty-two years I had been on the outside, throwing stones, fighting with megaphone in hand, campaigning, pointing the finger. Now, I was on the inside, not just on the inside of government in some ministerial position, but inside the beating heart of government.

It had been an incredible journey – a kid from St

Matthew's to a shower salesman to a ticket tout to an activist and now a player in No.10. But I had to watch my step and learn to be able to avoid bear traps, keep focused and be true to my core values. And it's that last part, core values that help you make the right decision, time after time. Yes, you want to get things done, and I would have to constantly compromise, but there were limits. Success at any price was not an option.

What I also witnessed in this all-encompassing, powerful place was that the power these people and the Party and the government have is rarely solid. That was particularly so with Theresa May, because from the moment she got in as prime minister the knives were out for her. I don't think there was ever a time when she felt the ground beneath her was remotely solid. It was very sad to see the great ambition she had very quickly ebb away, nevertheless, her vision was still strong and she would say that she wanted to make race equality policy announcements or other initiatives every three to four months: 'That's our goal,' she'd say. 'Drive policy for change.'

So I invented this role – Chair for the RDU Advisory community – for myself, and was backed and empowered by the prime minister. I asked for no money, as I strongly felt that an independent chair had to mean exactly that, and it couldn't if you were being paid. I also felt immensely privileged and honoured to serve my community first, and the wider society too. And it also allowed me as never before, and to understand the machinations of big politics.

At the top of our agenda was the Lammy Review, which was published in September 2017. An independent review, it looked into how Black, Asian and minority ethic individuals were treated in the Criminal Justice System and what the outcomes were for them. Ministers and civil servants came back with a comprehensive programme on delivering Lammy's recommendations. I was already familiar with Lammy's recommendations because I had been one of the report's advisors so I could wax lyrical on the big themes, about trust, about lack of representation, about the disparities in sentencing.

One of the most startling things the Lammy Review uncovered was the fact that in 2017, 40 per cent of youth incarceration was Black youths; three years later, that number had increased to 55 per cent. It's one thing to highlight this stuff, but quite another thing to have policies that are going to turn things around – and we just didn't. The truth of the matter is we just couldn't make the levers of government fundamentally tackle those disparities within the Criminal Justice system. To be fair to the civil servants, they at least had a programme that would help deliver, but when you have ministers that are not fully behind the programme, don't be surprised if the figures end up going in the wrong direction.

The other thing that I learned from being given this extraordinary role was that, either through the civil servants or directly through the SPADS, I could speak to ministers. I could write to them or I could pick up the phone and I'd say, I'm Simon Woolley, I need to speak to So-and-so. And they would call me back within twenty-four hours. This was a huge difference to what I'd been used to when I was campaigning or lobbying. Back then I'd get, 'I'm sorry, but that minister's busy for at least the next six months.' They may as well have just said; 'Piss off. He/she doesn't want to speak to you. Ever.'

But in the limited time and space that we had we were very ambitious, and nearly got a great deal done. In the end, on some of the big stuff you could say we failed, and to an extent I'd sadly accept that. But I don't apologise for trying, and I do hope that others can learn from my experiences. By the way, the successes are clear: The establishment of the Race Disparity Unit, still there today, the first of its kind in any modern democracy. The Youth foundation, a £100 million-plus body offering extraordinary support and a store of great knowledge in regards to what works in this area. My two big disappointments were around education, and employment, two key areas the PM said were her priorities too. We had concluded that to get systemic change that would tackle educational attainment, particularly in universities, the lack of Black professors, the curriculum and the widening participation agenda – you needed the strongest initiatives for all concerned to deliver that. The most effective tool that I witnessed was initiated by Dame Sally Davis, who was head of the medical association at the time, and is now a fellow Head of a Cambridge college – Trinity, which is arguably the most prestigious. She said, with the backing of government, that universities that signed up to the Athena Swan charter – which is the road map to tackle gender disparity within universities – would have a greater opportunity to receive significant funding, I think about £800 million. It's amazing how minds can change when the carrot of significant funding is on the table. From a very low take-up by universities of the Athena Swan gender programme, Davis managed to focus minds to get over a 90 per cent take-up with her just suggesting that universities would be seen in a more favourable light.

I thought, genius. No need to reinvent the wheel, just copy the model. I worked hard to join the dots and speak to all relevant people to get the comparable programme – The Race Equality Charter – which had a take-up of less than 10 per cent in the same space as Dame Sally did with Athena Swan. Nero and I had written the draft with great precision, and were waiting for the Cabinet Minister to make the announcement. I saw the announcement a day before it went live, and the critical line had been taken out. I was gutted. We – Nero and I – had turned our back for a second and that important line was taken out. I could have cried. And yes, I could have gone to the media, cried foul, got a headline, but we did get some things through, such as re-evaluating university league tables, and I also had other big things in play, such as the ethnic minority pay gap reporting. And in many ways, this was an even bigger deal.

The Prime Minister herself launched the consultation for ethnic minority pay-gap reporting with the clear guidance:

'This government must do this as we've done for gender.' Head of Mediacom, Karen Blackett, as well as banking leaders such as Head of Diversity Fiona Cannon and other business leaders were there to launch it. Surprisingly, for me, business leaders overwhelmingly backed the idea, as did civil society and the wider community. Everything was ready to go, but power was now ebbing away from No.10. The PM had set her departure date, and departments had dragged their feet, so the legislation was, as they say 'oven ready', but someone conveniently forgot to take it over the line. So there the 'oven ready' legislation sits, gathering dust with zero political will to implement transformation that would force big business – that is, only companies with 250 staff or more – to lay bare their ethnic minority pay gap. The race equality impetus that May started was not only halted by the incoming Johnson regime, but some within it seemed to make it their mission to take us back to a world in which racism was not only denied, but those talking about it would be demonised as enemies of the people.

It should be noted that as well was doing my No.10 role, I was still CEO of OBV with a myriad of all the wonderful projects we were undertaking, and I was constantly looking for the next big idea, which for me was the Colour of Power.

* * *

Back to 2016. I was at a transatlantic leadership retreat in Italy, attending a presentation by my dear friend, Dr Mischa Thompson, now the Director of Global Partnerships, at the

Transatlantic Inclusion Leadership Network, which we had founded together, along with some others. Mischa talked us through the ground-breaking work from the *New York Times* that had laid bare what American power looked like in their article titled 'The Faces of American Power, Nearly as White as the Oscar Nominees'. They took their cue from the Oscars 2015 'So white' debacle when no Black person was nominated that year. The *New York Times* piece undertook a powerful visual analysis from 500 powerful individuals to illustrate what power looked like in America, virtually an all-white and predominantly male array of faces.

Intrigued and excited about what I'd seen, I came back thinking we can do this, but better. If we are to understand the colour of power, I argued that we first we need to articulate power. What is power? What does it look like? Where does it lie? And from just a blank piece of paper we came up with about twenty-eight areas that we felt were significant to illustrate who were the people running the United Kingdom and what they looked like. Ashok's team spent the best part of six months pulling all this together, and finding the people who run these organisations. And after about 80 per cent of the work had been done, and I could see the shape of what we were going to say, I said, right, now we need a media partner. And so instinctively, we went to the *Guardian*, because they are a national newspaper rooted in social and racial justice

The *Guardian* took a big risk, backed by people who I'd worked with for twenty years including Hugh Muir and

Joseph Harker. In the end they threw the kitchen sink at this project, publishing in partnership with Operation Black Vote in September 2017. They had never done anything like it before. They gave about ten pages to this over the course of the week, including podcasts, and articles and many interviews. We laid bare the visual fact that at the top of who runs Britain – politics, business, the arts, the media – from over a list of over a thousand people in positions of power, only thirty-six were from Black, Asian and minority ethnic communities That's 3.4 per cent. And for women of colour, only seven held a position of power. Think of that. That's only 0.7 per cent. Less than 1 per cent. There were the outliers, like Edward Enninful, the editor of *Vogue*, or Perminder Mann, CEO of Bonnier Books UK – now my publishers. In 2017, of the top 40 unions there was not one black person at the top. There had not been a Black General Secretary since Bill Morris twenty years earlier. It seemed to me that in the UK, we are the entertainers, the footballers, the singers and the actors, but not seen as management material.

It is, of course, complicated. But at the end, what we were saying is that a person who was born in Britain as a Black, Asian, minority ethnic individual, in this trajectory you're virtually nowhere to be seen. And when people started asking questions within their companies, it was obvious that the pathway to the top level was almost all-white too. One of our best achievements from this project was that by looking at our list, you could extrapolate from that not only the colour of power, or the gender of power but also the class of power. Almost five years later, after the Black Lives Matter movement, the dial is changing. Not quick enough for my liking, but it's moving in the right direction. From thirty-six people from Black, Asian and minority ethnic communities at the top to double that – seventy-eight. Such is the interest in The Colour of Power, our African American friends want some of the action too. It looks like The Colour of power – in the US, the Color of Power – just went international.

*   *   *

I'm sorry that I jump around a bit – things aren't always linear, right?

As we ended the year in 2019, a number of big elements occurred that would have huge consequences for the UK. Boris Johnson had taken over from Theresa May and had won a landslide election in December 2019. Jeremy Corbyn's wheels had come off, big time. An Eton-educated Bullingdon boy had won the hearts and minds of working-class people up in the North of England, in the Midlands, a particularly astounding feat, aided in no small measure by the Brexit narrative that meant a lot to many working areas.

The right-wing populist movement headed up by Nigel Farage had momentum – monstrous, often poisonous, xenophobic momentum – which was sweeping the UK. The Labour Party and Jeremy Corbyn, in particular, had played such a poor game during the whole of the Brexit debate, which was why they found themselves in no man's land, neither for it nor really against him. This indecision and dithering opened the door for Boris Johnson to lean into that xenophobic strain, rather than push back against it, as Scottish leader Nicola Sturgeon did, with his rhetoric of 'I hear your concerns. This is about Britain, this is about you, I've got your back,' and they clearly sided with him and voted for him in huge numbers.

I've always tried to find a common ground with political leaders, build trust with them, to foster conversation, to work out actions in our mutual interest. But with the present PM it's always been tough. This little encounter illustrates this.

At every mayoral election, Operation Black Vote holds hustings meetings and in 2008, we held a meeting in the Kingsway Church in West London. All the candidates were there – Ken Livingstone, Boris Johnson and the Liberal Democrats. Pastor Nims Obunge of the Freedom's Ark church in Tottenham and CEO of The Peace Alliance and me were the hosts. Someone asked Boris Johnson a question about all his racist remarks – 'flag-waving piccaninnies', which he wrote in a 2002 *Daily Telegraph* article, is just one example of many. Johnson gave some waffle of an answer and Pastor Nims said, 'OK, all right.' But I said, 'Stop, stop, stop, stop, stop!' I walked on, took the mic from Pastor Nims and said, 'Boris, that's not an answer. I'm going to ask you one more time about this,' and his face was like thunder. I never let him off, though, and he looked at me as if he was thinking, *I'll get you, you bastard*. He squirmed and squirmed and squirmed.

Anyway, fast forward two years and my friend Raminder Singh Ranger, Baron Ranger, a Tory donor, was organising an event for Boris Johnson and I was invited. Not just invited, I had been seated right next to Boris Johnson himself. Johnson arrives late, coming through the door like a rock star. Rami goes out to meet him and when Johnson sees who he's sitting next to, I can see him mumbling under his breath, 'Fucking hell!' So, I'm thinking what can I do now? My easiest option is to get up, make some sorry-ass excuse and leave. A three-hour dinner is a long time with someone you really don't want to be next to. And he made that abundantly clear. Or should I do what I'd normally do – try to make the best of a bad situation? I chose the latter option. He sits down, he's polite, but cold. My response to him is, 'Boris, can I say one thing?' I can see him bristling but continue – 'What you wrote in the *Evening Standard* the other week was sheer genius.' 'What was that? What did I write, what did I write?' he said and I said, 'You wrote that you wanted to give amnesty to those seeking asylum, "give them citizenship", you said, and get them to pay taxes. It's a genius move, that is the type of progressive mayor we need,' I said. 'I knew, Simon, you were a good guy,' and then he relaxed and we had a pleasant evening.

But here's the thing, I was drained, but what I understood was that for him to listen to me, I had to park the awful things he said about Black people, such as 'watermelon smiles', and show not only good grace and decency, but make him feel comfortable.

Without sounding arrogant, I can persuasively articulate

and illustrate why tackling persistent race inequality is a good thing for everyone, and most people will understand me, take what I say on board. But you don't stand a chance if the psychological shutters are down.

* * *

By early January 2020, I knew that my days were numbered as chair of the Race Disparity Unit Advisory Group. Samuel Kasumu had taken over from Nero Ughwujabo after Theresa May lost her leadership battle. I had originally encouraged Samuel to take the job, because I thought well, Nero brought him in, I had supported him. I knew he was a very decent guy. In January, he asked me to meet with him. I knew the writing was on the wall. When I entered the room, all eyes were on the floor.

'Look, I know my days are numbered,' I said. 'Just make sure that the unit survives.'

'Simon, it's been made clear to me through Munira Mirza [his then Head of Policy] that Boris Johnson that he wants people who are demonstrably "his". These are his exact words. And we know you're no one's much less his.'

'One hundred per cent. Don't even sweat it,' I said to him. 'As long as we get a good transition.'

The funny thing about the Race Disparity Unit is that its biggest detractor when we launched in 2017 was Munira Mirza, now head of policy. She was all over the airwaves, saying if you talk about racism, more racism will exist. The Racial Disparity Unit is a waste of time and blah, blah, blah,

blah, blah. And she was everywhere. Now, she concluded that actually, the Race Disparity Unit is useful.

That's interesting. Why the change of heart? I thought. I soon found out because you've got a unit that gathers evidence, how you use that evidence, how you cherry pick, it can be something completely different. Mirza and our team thought, *Actually, we can use this for our political agenda.* And they did, and how.

But this was the beginning of 2020, and we all know what the main issue of 2020 was …

Covid.

* * *

In June 2020, the UK and many parts of the rest of the world were in turmoil. The death rate from Covid-19 was growing day by day and fear and anxiety were taking hold. What was particularly alarming at home in the UK were mass and social media montages of the victims' portraits. When the images of healthcare workers were displayed, the faces of those on the frontline of saving and caring for the British public were full of African, Caribbean and Asian sub-continent workers: doctors, nurses, care home workers, porters and cleaners. Of the first wave of doctors who had died, 97 out of 100 were from our communities. In the general population of those who were dying disproportionately, there were bus drivers, taxi drivers and security guards – once again, frontline workers that Black and Asian people in the UK hold in significant numbers.

For those who cared or dared to look, it wasn't rocket science to piece together the key factors that would help explain who and why certain ethnic communities were dying in much greater numbers: those of African and Caribbean descent were four times more likely to die than white people, with Asians a close second at three times more likely to die. All these ethnic groups were equally more likely to be overly exposed to this vicious disease. A lack of protective clothing or shielding, coupled with many on low-paid, zero-hour contracts, working in those front-facing public spaces made these individuals extremely vulnerable to this deadly virus. And whilst 90 per cent of the nation was safer as we locked down, those low-paid workers had little or no option but work in so many unsafe areas – buses, care homes, hospitals – so that they could pay their rent and feed their children.

What this disease did was to lay bare the structural racial fault lines in society. Follow the disease and it would expose societal areas of gross inequality. In that fact, it was an extraordinary disease.

What I was able to see was that there were spaces in our society that we can best describe as racialised; which means that in these areas of our society, racial inequality is writ large, whether it be in jobs, housing inequality, health or education.

All these factors were being played out in the pandemic. One Saturday morning, while tuning in to Radio 4, I listened to the Headmaster of Eton College, Simon Henderson, discussing how the pandemic was potentially the biggest crisis in the history of Britain's education system, but he also suggested that it presented perhaps its greatest opportunity for change. If we're not careful, Henderson said, a generation of disadvantaged young people, particularly those from Black, Asian and minority ethnic communities, would fall irretrievably behind because of this pandemic. He added that it was incumbent upon us to acknowledge this deficit and do something about it. To address the deficit, Eton College would provide £100 million to ensure students who were disadvantaged didn't fall further behind because such educational inequality wasn't good for society.

What I liked about what Henderson said, and I would shamelessly steal his lines in the hundreds of talks I did around this time, was the line that 'historians would look back at this period, this age of Covid, and ask but one question: with inequalities laid brutally bare, how did we respond to what the pandemic was screaming at us?' This pandemic, for all its horrors, had given us the greatest opportunity to acknowledge and put right the structural inequalities that were there way before this disease unleashed itself. I kept saying to anyone who would listen, that this was potentially a 1945 moment: Not 'build back better', which was the refrain at the time, but build new better. I honestly felt that this was a moment for us to dive deep and honestly into confronting structural inequalities.

The death of Emanuel Gomes was one of many tragic cases that illustrates the degree to which race and occupation have been a factor when it comes to the unnecessary deaths of ethnic minorities from Covid. Employed as a Home Office zero-hours contract cleaner, Emanuel was forced to continue working even after he'd started feeling ill. In the early days of the pandemic, so many people just like Emanuel, people with job insecurity and instability who form a rapidly growing class known as the 'precariat', continued to work while unwell instead of resting because they felt they had little choice. In Emanuel's case, this lack of choice proved fatal. After finishing his shift on 24 April 2020, he fell ill and died of Covid. Like many other low-paid or zero-hour workers, Emanuel knew he would not get statutory sick pay unless he worked. But anecdotes aside, the facts were clear: we were more likely to catch the disease, more likely to be seriously ill by it and ultimately more likely to die from it. And that was also true in the US too. If ever I needed an incentive to do the work I have dedicated most of my life to, it was this and the time was now.

In politics, timing is everything. And it was shocking timing to have this government in power at this time of national crisis in regards to acknowledging and effectively tackling systemic racism.

Key people in government, in particular Head of Policy Munira Murza, were deniers of systemic race inequality way before the pandemic was unleashed. I had thought, hoped, that the evidence was so strong, so irrefutable, that they would have a change of heart. No. Mirza and others doubled down and pushed back hard.

Dr Tony Sewell, who would ultimately be the

government's systemic race inequality denier, wrote in *The Times* in April 2020 an astonishing and gut-wrenching opinion piece stating that rather than look at social determinates we should look at the genetics to find the answer why Black people were dying in greater numbers. He referred to me as a 'flat earth thinker' for suggesting social determinates were the biggest factor in racial inequality. The horror of such crude analysis to a community who knew this genetic analysis was a slippery slope towards the racist eugenics who were never far away.

I wasn't bothered about the insults, I'd been called much worse. But I was incandescent with rage that instead of the dealing with the systemic problem that had led many to die, we were in effect being blamed for it. It's our genetics. My blood boils even now as I remember what was unfolding.

* * *

When the UK government suggested they would undertake a review by Public Health England into the disproportionate deaths in the BAME (Black, Asian and minority ethnic) community from coronavirus, the veteran broadcaster and former head of the Commission for Equality and Human Rights, Trevor Phillips was widely trailed as the man who should take the helm.

He had publicly applauded Sewell's genetics piece, but had also made his own pronouncement that Bangladeshi and Pakistani people were not dying in disproportionate numbers because, they wash their 'hands five times a day' before prayer. Fact is, they were dying at shocking rates, in spite of their handwashing. But again, rather than confront an uncomfortable truth that laid bare the accumulative effects of poor housing, inequality in health, intergenerational housing (that was not always aligned with poverty) and overcrowding, the fact that they weren't dying in even greater numbers was down to 'washing hands'? As soon as Phillips' name was in the frame many eyebrows were raised in Black, Asian and ethnic minority communities, but of course from the government's perspective he, like Sewell, was a good fit. 'Avoid acknowledging much less accepting systemic race inequality at all cost', seemed to be the government's mantra. And some couldn't wait to be its cheerleaders.

I couldn't believe our bad luck. We had this once-in-a-lifetime chance to really change the system and it was being squandered. Worse still, the government were finding people like us to do their bidding.

Therefore, I had one of the biggest dilemmas of my political life to date: I could either sit on my hands and do nothing, or do what I'd never done before, which was to call a Black brother out in public. Truth is, I had no option if I was to be driven by my values. I felt I was not alone and encouraged by the fact that hundreds of nurses and doctors had written open letters calling for Phillips' removal from the Inquiry. My dear friend the writer Afua Hirsch also made a public stand against the trajectory that Phillips and others were taking. So I said, 'Look, it's not personal, although to Phillips it will seem personal.' I knew that. But I had to say that Phillips was not the man to head up this Health Commission because at this point he simply was not trusted by the people who needed help and, until he built that trust, until he demonstrated that the people could trust him, he shouldn't do it. So I wrote the article with my good friend Baroness Warsi, who had also been worried about where this was going, particularly for Bangladeshi and Pakistani communities. I thought it was a balanced article, even if the headline 'With Trevor Phillips involved, the BAME coronavirus inquiry will struggle to gain trust' was not to my liking and a bit too dramatic, but it built up enough steam for people to say, actually, Phillips has been on the wrong side of these arguments for some time now and we have to defend our communities. In the end, the government chose Professor Kevin Fenton, a brilliant man who objectively looked at the medical and social determinant evidence and produced a balanced report the government all but disowned.

In regards to Trevor Phillips, we haven't spoken since, but I hope we do some day. Friends should be able to respectfully disagree.

* * *

A month after Emanuel Gomes died, in America, May 2020, another global pandemic began to emerge. This time, however, it was of a societal and cultural nature rather than a virus driven one.

The brutal and shocking murder of forty-six-year-old

African-American George Floyd at the hands of, or in his case, the knee of Minneapolis police officer Derek Chauvin, sent shockwaves around the world because it was captured on a mobile phone by a bystander. To date, I still can't bring myself to watch the full nine minutes and twenty-nine seconds of horror on that video, the killing of a man pleading for his life, asking for his mother before he died. This was not the first and it certainly won't be the last case of a Black man dying in horrific circumstances. Still, it was the straw that broke the camel's back: the response to this all-too-familiar modern tragedy was a global one that galvanised a mass direct action movement. The rebirth of Black Lives Matter.

The millions who then took to the streets after the video of George Floyd went viral understood acutely that it wasn't just Derek Chauvin's knee that killed Mr Floyd but the American system of deep race inequality. This system too often would give the green light for law enforcement officers to use lethal force for the most minor infringements by African-Americans and consistently delivers unequal outcomes across the matrix of American society.

In the wake of George Floyd's killing, America exploded with unrest. Black Britons were also well aware that innocuous interactions between Black people and the police could prove fatal.

Through the resurgence of Black Lives Matter, protestors demanded deep and systemic change. For example, British Hollywood star John Boyega joined tens of thousands in

Hyde Park, London to demand we confront these inequalities in jobs, housing, education, health and the Criminal Justice system in the UK. Protestors demanded that where racial inequality has been systemically baked into our institutions, it must be confronted, challenged and effectively dealt with. The easy targets for this symbolism were the statues of enslavers of kidnapped Africans. A notorious example is Bristol's Edward Colston, who for centuries was revered for his philanthropy while the dark side of his deeds, including throwing enslaved Africans into the sea to save his overcrowded ship, and claim on the insurance, were swept under the carpet. And to be clear it wasn't just about the symbolic nature of the statues, the statues were often on, or closely connected to, the institutions that had in their DNA a narrative of white supremacy.

Just as I'd hoped, the debates sparked by the Black Lives Matter movement and Covid crisis were starting up a lot of great, if uncomfortable conversations in our society.

Now was the opportunity to have the greatest conversation in British history about race equality. Black Lives Matter and Covid had created the perfect storm. In this country, we'd barely spoken about the roots of slavery, the roots of colonialism, until statues were being torn down and questions were being asked by so many more people. People seemed receptive to change.

People started talking about taking a long hard look at our curriculum to better understand how its DNA was in part perpetuating a cultural superiority that was harmful for everyone. It wasn't rewriting history, it was better understanding it. History can make tough reading, but reading and understanding with an open mind is surely what our education should be about. On the business side, many CEOs were listening as never before to their Black staff and hearing horror stories – for example, a Black person would train a white person, only for that white staffer to get promoted above the Black person, becoming they're boss. Before the BLM protests, Black staff wouldn't even speak out. Now their bosses, who had assumed they were 'right on' liberal business leaders, were shocked to their core as to what they were hearing. I sat in on quite of few of these meetings and I watched grown men cry. Many already had an inclination that something was wrong – all they had to do was glance at their all-white boards, their nearly all-white senior staff. But astonishingly, many were up for a conversation about how we put things right. I'd never witnessed such heartfelt conversation before. And I'm still not sure if this momentum will last, it feels as if its already dwindling, but conversation and plans to put things right are definitely occurring.

* * *

I've mentioned before the 'system justification', a theory of cognitive dissonance. The theory is, in order to get on in life you learn how to ignore societal prejudices and disadvantages, both institutional and personal, that allows you cut through the obstacles and problems that can ordinarily hold you back or weigh you down. To some extent I get that but only if you're consciously ignoring these obstacles, rather than in denial of them.

The government's response to the hundreds of thousands who took to the streets to demand greater racial justice was the Sewell Report. It was published on 31 March 2021, nine months after the death of George Floyd

My heart sunk when Sewell and the reports headlines hit the airwaves: 'Institutional racism no longer exits' – the UK is a 'model country' when comes to race, the report said, BLM protestors and their 'well-meaning idealism' were patronised as shockingly naïve. And Sewell had something up his sleeve to ward off those pesky 'decolonise the curriculum' campaigners with this 'positive' spin on the enslavement of millions of Africans:

'There is a new story about the Caribbean experience which speaks to the slave period not only being about profit and suffering but how culturally African people transformed themselves into a remodelled African/Britain.'

I'm guessing then, that someone like me who, along with millions of others had our names, cultures and much of our histories erased to be replaced by something very British is a good story about slavery?

The Sewell report has been the worst report in modern British history by a long measure. In fact, it's one of the greatest endorsements of state-endorsed gaslighting many of us had ever seen.

In times of plenty with racial inequalities extremely low,

he might have got away with this, but this was in response to Black Lives Matter, the nation's moment to be profoundly honest, not shockingly dishonest.

In the end, what did for Sewell and his report, were the doctors, lawyers, academics, NGO campaigners, and the Church, all of whom gave evidence to his commission, denouncing it as a wilful misrepresentation of the facts and a lost opportunity to move the race inequality dial forward.

Ironically, the Sewell Report did show one thing accurately – it showed how racism works. Black, Asian and minority communities are too often not believed, and that governments can weaponise Black people to say and do the things they themselves couldn't say without being called a racist.

* * *

The American civil rights activist Al Sharpton talks about the journey, the continual journey forward. We're learning on the way, that's all we can ever do. We're regrouping and this period will be seen as significant because it's been challenging the pushback we've had. We've had pushback from Donald Trump, from Boris Johnson with Tony Sewell, but thankfully the latter as been broadly defeated.

Because of Covid -19 and Black Lives Matter the nation has never been so ready for great change, and the UK government could have leaned in, as others have done, to help the progress towards a more equitable society.

But the government has chosen not to engage seriously

so we've stalled. The Omicron variant and now this ghastly unprovoked war in the Ukraine, will blow us off track even more. But we must return to these very big conversations, because it'll help enormously as we go into the future.

CHAPTER 10

BLACK FACES IN HIGH PLACES

On 7 July 2005, while, like most people in London, I was calling around, trying to make sure that none of my friends and family, or any of Operation Black Vote's employees or volunteers, had been caught up in the four terrorist bombs that went off that morning, I received a letter. It was an extraordinary juxtaposition. While chaos reigned in central London, a very official-looking document, which I half expected would inform me that because of an unpaid parking fine or other infringement I'd be off to the Tower for a indeterminate prison sentence, arrived It looked that official, but the letter from No.10 Downing Street was something pleasantly different, informing me that the Prime Minister Tony Blair would like to offer me the prestigious award of the Order of the British Empire. In the same year they had given one to the football hero David Beckham. Just trying to give some perspective here.

The reason for this very unexpected overture, the letter said, was on account of my work on race equality. It was somewhat jaw-dropping, to say the least, and it led to one of the most profound political questions I've ever confronted in my life. I had spent ten years fighting systemic racism and trying to empower our communities. My son was about to be born a month later. Now, the Prime Minister wanted to offer me an award for that work. What's not to like? Could I, in all honesty, take an award in the name of the British Empire? After all, wasn't I a product of it? Yeah, but that's not the point. The endeavour of the Empire was not to produce Simon Woolley, or even Lord Woolley of Woodford. It was to exploit resources, for the financial benefit of the UK, by any means necessary. And I mean, any means.

It certainly didn't feel it was something to celebrate. On the other hand, the letter was saying that we want to celebrate your achievements to our society. There's an impossible tension for many of us. Can we celebrate our life's work in the name of the Empire? It's a personal choice, which is made more difficult for many of us descendants of people from the Commonwealth, particularly those brought over to work.

I also felt strongly that if it wasn't right, I needed to know that I could say no. For me, it wasn't just the word 'Empire' that was deeply challenging, it was about me being able to challenge it. Over those ten years or more, I'd seen politicians not speaking out. They'd say to me, 'Simon, wait until I get that senior role, then you'll hear me.' And then they'd get there and the silence would be deafening.

The problem, I reasoned, begins when you start making excuses because you want to say yes; because you want the bauble, the recognition, the slap on the back. You could even frame it as a victory for our people, as 'the Empire strikes back', if you like, but what you're really doing is pandering to your fragile ego and ignoring your own sense of what's right and wrong. Let me make this clear too, not everyone even acknowledges this tension, much less wrestles with it, but many do, and they shouldn't have to. Change 'Empire' to 'Excellence' and you lose nothing but include everyone.

I spoke to my dear friends and of course they all said take it, you *must* take it. An OBE is a serious honour. My friend and mentor for many years Hugh Harris said to me, 'Listen, Simon, you have to take it because in the British system there's a trajectory: you get the OBE, then you get a CBE, then you get a knighthood.' I thought about his angle on it but I realised that I wouldn't be able to accept it. Two years earlier, the poet Benjamin Zephaniah had turned down the OBE and was very vocal in his refusal, which was covered by almost every newspaper. I thought to myself, *I have to decline but I'm not going to make a big fuss about it.* I absolutely see why Benjamin did it – as a very well-known person, he drew attention to the problem of the honours system – but for me, I felt it could be just another way to say, 'Oh, look at me! I've been awarded a gong! I'm just not going to take it …' It could be another way of pandering to my inner ego.

So I wrote to the Prime Minister, telling him that my mother had long since died but that she would have been the proudest woman on God's planet to see her son from a council estate being awarded a great honour by Her Majesty the Queen. However, as an activist fighting for social and racial justice I could not, with all conscience, take an honour that celebrates the Empire. I urged the Prime Minister to rethink the honours system and find a way that the word 'Empire' could be removed and perhaps replaced with the 'Order of British Excellence', or words to that effect, as recommended by a report to the government in 2004.

People need to be recognised for their work but they shouldn't have to choke down the word 'Empire'. A reward from your country should be about excellence, that's a no brainer. It's my view that there was nothing good about the British Empire. Anyone who says, 'But hang on a minute, we should marvel at the railways, the democratic infrastructures and the "civilising" influence that the Empire built,' I would answer them: 'Ask a Jewish person if they would say, "At least the Nazi regime built fantastic autobahns."' If there were plenty of positive elements about Empire then I don't think that the Democratic Republic of Congo, which is one of the richest countries on the planet in terms of mineral wealth, would also be the poorest, in economic terms. The DRC is no longer part of the Belgian Empire but it's a world order that continues to exploit its teeming rich resources, including rubber, gold, copper and cobalt – a component in mobile phone batteries.

To be fair to Tony Blair, his government did explore a change in the titles but then the *Daily Mail* got wind of it and all hell broke loose. What I've learned about politics, particularly high-level politics, is that politicians do care hugely what the media says and the *Daily Mail* is probably, sadly, at the top of the list. When deciding on a course of action, or which position to take, many politicians ask themselves, 'What would the *Daily Mail* say?' There are not many politicians bold enough or brave enough to take it on, unnecessarily, as they see it, provoking this powerful right-wing paper's wrath can wreak havoc on an MP's career.

I told very few people about the letter from No.10 and my decision. However, I did tell our chair at Operation Black Vote, Rita Patel, and it turned out that she had refused a CBE for very similar reasons of principle and had never told a soul. She said, 'Isn't it extraordinary? Two kids from council estates in Leicester being awarded honours and quietly refusing.' Though I would now love to see Rita recognised for the work that she's done for thirty years for Black women and Asian women, and for our communities around the country in general. She has achieved some remarkable things.

* * *

At the beginning of 2019, I was dealing with a kaleidoscope of projects, both at home and abroad. The Race Disparity Unit was now well established and something I was very proud of. I was working on the Open Society Foundation in New York, US and in Berlin, Germany, and on the Transatlantic Leaders Network in Europe. Operation Black Vote was stronger than ever, with a presence right across the country. However, nationally, all anyone could talk about was Brexit. Early in 2019, Theresa May's government was defeated three times when Parliament voted against ratifying the withdrawal agreement. By the end of May, she would have stepped down as prime minister.

A few weeks before this happened, around 5 May, I got another very official-looking letter through the door, from the Cabinet Office. I opened it up. The inside was headed 'In Confidence' and said: 'the Prime Minister has asked me to inform you that, on the advice of the main honours committee, she is recommending that Her Majesty The Queen may be graciously pleased to approve that the honour of knighthood be conferred upon you in the birthday 2019 Honours List.' I was speechless – something that, as many of my good friends and colleagues will tell you, does not happen to me, almost ever. The citation was particularly special: 'Simon Woolley has helped to transform our society by ensuring the nation's Black, Asian and minority ethnic communities positively engage in civic society and politics and make the UK a better place to live.'

Unbeknown to me, the Cabinet Office had been in

liaison with my deputy, Ashok Viswanathan. They knew that I had turned down the OBE fourteen years earlier and wanted to try and find out if I would accept the knighthood, given that there are few of these high-end honours to give out each year. They were concerned that I would turn round and say no, as I did before. Ashok made it clear that he believed if there was any notion of the Empire in the honour bestowed on me that I would not take it. So rather than CBE, which stands for Commander of the Most Excellent Order of the British Empire, and which many people who have been knighted have after their name, I would simply be 'Kt', meaning a 'Knight Bachelor'. This harks back to the early Middle Ages, rather than being an order created in the time of Empire.

I was over the moon. To be offered such a high honour for making my country a better place to live – well, I don't think it gets any better than that. I felt like I wanted to walk out of the house, climb on my roof and shout, 'I'm going to be made a knight. A Black knight!' I kept thinking of Sir Elton John, Sir Simon Rattle, Sir Mick Jagger, Sir Ben Kingsley . . . and then Sir Simon Woolley. I couldn't believe it. The letter explained that the announcement would be in June, when the Birthday Honours List is published, which was about a month or so away. Keeping that close to my chest was a challenge indeed!

Things were going great in many ways. Later, when the announcement was made, I did some interviews with the press, including Kay Burley on Sky News. Having been roasted so many times in the past by the broadcast media, this interview was a joy. Still hardly able to believe it myself, I said, 'It's not supposed to happen to people like me. I'm from St Matthew's, a tough working-class council estate. I left school with no O-levels, no A-levels. And I'm going to be knighted . . .'

But meanwhile, in government, Brexit had destroyed the Cabinet and was about to destroy the career of Theresa May. We were desperately worried about the Race Disparity Unit and what would happen to it in the long term. For some months now, what with everything else that was going on, it had been mothballed and restricted from doing what it was designed to do. A lot of people were worried about would happen to their projects. I spoke to Gavin Barwell, Theresa May's chief of staff, who agreed to meet me.

My first question was, 'How's the Prime Minister? How is she bearing up with all of this? It looks like things are going to come to an end pretty soon.'

'Thank you for asking, Simon. I'm worried about the Prime Minister, too. This is a woman who, as you know, gets up at four or five in the morning. She's driven to do what she can and she's not been able to do what she really wanted to do because Brexit is taking the lifeblood out of government.'

We talked about the Race Disparity Unit and some other things, including Nero Ughwujabo, who had been a loyal foot soldier. I said that if there was anything I could do, I'd do it, but I would recommend that he be elevated to the House of Lords because he was a very decent guy and a good advocate for everything we cared about. I also expressed concern for Samuel Kasumu, who I thought had been doing some great work as part of the Race Disparity Unit.

This must have been around 12 or 13 May, around two weeks before the Prime Minister resigned. A week after that meeting, I received perhaps the most extraordinary call in my life, ever. I was sat at my desk in Bethnal Green when the phone rang: 'Could I speak to Simon Woolley, please.'

I answered fairly brusquely: 'Who is it?'

'It's Gavin Barwell.'

'Gavin, how are you, man? Sorry. Just recently, we've been getting some very, very horrible, racist calls, so I have to be careful about how I answer.'

Gavin said, 'Simon, let me tell you this. This really isn't a hateful call. On the contrary. The Prime Minister has asked me to ask you if you would accept being elevated to the House of Lords.'

I had to catch my breath. It was one of those moments in which it's difficult to compute exactly what has just been said to you. Had I been standing up I would have had to sit down, immediately. I stuttered. I didn't know whether to laugh, cry, I was just so full of emotion.

Gavin continued, 'We've been thinking about this for some time. But it was extraordinary to us that in the last days of the Prime Minister's role, when people were coming in to ask about themselves and their careers, you were asking for other people. We knew you were the right person to elevate for this role.'

I think I managed to get across that I was honoured and thrilled, but I'd guess I was slightly incoherent. I mean, you would be after a government officer, out of the blue, calls you up – that is one of those life-changing moments. And to mess up my equilibrium I had still not fully come to terms with being a Sir. And now, in the same month, I was told that I was going to be a lord. I thanked him profusely and said yes, yes, I'd be honoured, and could he please thank the PM, a lot, a great deal. Thank you.

I put the phone down and sat back in my chair, thinking, *Oh my God, oh my God, oh God, this is surreal.* And then another wave of horror came flooding over me: *Oh my gosh, they think I'm a Tory! They want to make me a Conservative peer because we worked so well together. Oh no! I can't, I won't. Not even for a Peerage.* I kept thinking I would have to say no like I did in 2005 for the OBE. Being non-partisan had always been so important, so integral to what I had been able to achieve. I could not pretend to be a Conservative because it afforded me a life-changing title. I was bitterly disappointed, of course, but I knew that I couldn't do that. *Oh well,* I told myself, *I'll have to remain just a regular old sir.*

I should have just rung them up to ask but I was worried that it would look too ungracious. Anyway, a few days later I was still planning how to broach the subject and turn down a Conservative peerage when I got another call from the

Prime Minister's office. They said, 'We're just sorting out the detail and you'll need to go to the Garter's office to find the place where you want to be the Lord, as a crossbench peer.' *Yes, yes, yes!* I was metaphorically cartwheeling around the office.

So much had happened in such a short time that it was already hard to take in and I was almost wondering what other bombshells might be in store every time I picked up the phone. Then, in the September, lo and behold, a call came from Buckingham Palace, no less.

'Sir Simon …' – that sounded good coming from Buckingham Palace – 'we understand that in a few months' time you will be ennobled as Lord Woolley.'

'Yes, that's correct.'

The official said, 'Well, if you're a lord, then you cannot be officially knighted. It doesn't mean that you lose your title or it's eradicated but hierarchy dictates a lord cannot be knighted.'

I asked the official, 'What does that mean? Does that mean that I won't get my day at Buckingham Palace?'

'Yes,' he said. 'That is the case. Unless we can fit you in before your ennoblement.'

I was due to be knighted in January 2020. That was my official date.

The official said, 'Can you come to the Palace next week?'

'Erm, erm … Yes, I think, I mean I know we can do that.' And so there was a mad rush to get organised. Three people are allowed to come to the investiture. Of course,

I wanted my son, number one priority. And his mum, my long-term partner, but now one of my best friends. And my birth mother, Lolita.

I called Lolita in Leicester: 'Would you like to come?'

'I would love to,' she replied, 'but I'm not quite sure how I'm going to get down.'

She'd been having awful problems with her knees, hips and back. Having been a nurse for all her adult life at a time when safe lifting procedures and protocols were virtually non-existent, like all nurses then, my mum would lift patients in and out of bed, and bathe them, and all this had taken its toll on her body. Plus, she'd just had an operation and really couldn't get the train, so I gave her a couple of options.

'I'm happy to drive up to Leicester, pick you up and then take you back. Alternatively, I could get a limousine to get you, bring you to the Palace and then wait and take you back. We'll have dinner afterwards.'

She agreed. But then, at the last minute, she said, 'Simon, I can't do it. I just can't do it, I'm just too unwell. And I don't want to detract from your day.'

Of course I said it wouldn't, but that was what she wanted. She just didn't feel physically strong enough. And while I was a little bit sad, I was OK with it. Ideally, I would have wanted both my mothers there to see me knighted at Buckingham Palace.

* * *

The tenth of October 2019, the day of the investiture, was a glorious day. Luca had chosen a suit, which he wanted to wear with a black polo neck and white shoes. No tie for him, he didn't need one. He looked very cool. We arrived at the Palace and were directed to a long hallway. Luca's mum went to the ladies', leaving the two of us standing there, awed, in this great long corridor by ourselves. Luca ran a little way down, ran back and jumped into my arms.

'Dad, we're at the Palace!'

To him, it was like a scene from a movie – actually, it was for me too.

Then I was shown into the rooms where they talk you through what you have to do and explain the protocols, like don't turn your back on the Queen. You don't actually know very far in advance who will be giving you the honour. It could be the Prince of Wales, the Duke of Cambridge or the Princess Royal. I had hoped it might be the Queen and was very pleased when I found out that it would be.

If you're being knighted, you're first in line in the ceremony. There were about four or five other people in front of me and then I got a nod from the official to come forward. It was a surreal moment. All of us, in this country particularly but all around the world too, we've seen the Queen on TV, on our currency, on our stamps – her image is so familiar. And then you come face to face with the person you've known all your life. But who of course you don't know.

There was a little stool in front of her where I had

been briefed to place one knee and then the Queen raised the sword. With a knighthood, she doesn't actually say the 'arise' thing, that's a bit of a myth, but she does put the sword on your shoulder. What was also amazing was that on the stage next to the Queen there was a young Black man dressed immaculately in a ceremonial palace uniform. Whenever anybody came up, it was his job to whisper to the Queen, I guess telling her who it was. Something is also read out to explain what your award is for.

After Her Majesty had given me the medal, known as an insignia (you get a special pin to wear beforehand, for the Queen to hang it from), she said, 'So, Simon, you've been doing great work with race equality and we're very grateful. What are you working on next?'

I said that I was working on voter registration for the next election. She said something like 'Good luck, there.' Or, 'You need all the luck there, you've got your work cut out.' Or something like that.

And I said, 'You bet I will!' And then we both laughed.

Then you have you walk backwards and then exit. At that point, I saw Luca sitting at the end of a row, stretching his neck like a giraffe to take everything in, as he saw his dad been knighted by Her Majesty The Queen. Afterwards, he said, 'Dad, Dad … What did you say to the Queen to make her laugh?'

'I can't tell you, son,' I replied. 'It's a state secret.' He threw me a couple of jokey punches for that!

The whole ceremony was over in a couple of hours. It's

amazing that the Queen stood there for all that time. It was a great day.

We went out into the Palace courtyard, where there was an archway, through which we could see crowds of tourists outside. We've all been there. You go to Buckingham Palace and you've got your head pressed up against the railings. And as we came out, people were pointing at Luca, looking at me and taking pictures. God knows who they thought he was! Of course, I enjoyed it for him, though I was still a bit overwhelmed myself. And I enjoyed the day for my mother, too. For both my mothers, but I was thinking a lot about my mothers, in particular, Pippi. I thought she'd be proud and I wished she could have seen it. Her boy, who had once dressed in the clothes given to us by the mothers of kids she looked after, who couldn't afford to pay her any other way, wearing a suit and emerging into the London sunshine, having just been given an award by the Queen. So much of who I am, what took me from Leicester on that incredible journey to Buckingham Palace, was down to her.

* * *

The most extraordinary thing was that just nine days later, I was due to be ennobled at the House of Lords.

So in barely more than a week, I was going from ordinary citizen to knight to lord of the realm. As one of my close friends put it, 'Simon, you've gone from serf to sir to lord.' We wondered if that would qualify me for the Guinness

World Records; surely that had to be the shortest time in British history? My official title would be Lord Simon Woolley of Woodford, Kt. I remember going to the Garter's office – he's the one who wears garters and breeches and an intricately embroidered tunic with gold insignia everywhere. Less formally attired in his office, he asked me where I wanted to associate my title. I did think about my council estate Leicester, or where I lived in Woodford, London. But I said to the Garter, what about 'Lord Woolley of Everywhere? I imagined in my mind the Speaker announcing, Lord Woolley of Everywhere to speak.' With a wry smile, the Garter informed me that I had to be a little more geographically specific. So I chose the place where I lived the longest, Woodford. If it was good enough for Prime Minister Winston Churchill, it's good enough for me.

On 19 October, we trooped off to the House of Lords for another incredible formal ceremony. I had asked my best friend Gary, who was living in Panama, to come. He happily agreed to fly over but wanted to make one condition: that I wouldn't wear a robe with ermine, as Gary is a committed vegetarian. 'Consider it done,' I said. Though a part of me was worried that it might not be that easy on the day, as there are actually only about four robes made with fake fur and the rest are ermine. Luckily, I got one of them.

All the new peers processed into the Grand Hall for the Ceremony of Introduction. My family were up in the galleries with my closest friends, Gary, Gabby and Savvas, my old friend from Leicester, with their wives. Luca was hanging over the balcony in a state of wonder at it all. In the hall, there are a couple of seats near the throne where the Queen sits for the State Opening of Parliament. Sitting there, I saw the now former Prime Minister, Theresa May. She watched the whole ceremony, beaming with pride, secure in the knowledge that I would respect and use the role to further racial and social justice.

With the ceremony done, we traipsed off for photographs. I was the first to arrive. I had a whole range of pictures with my sponsors – the two lords who traditionally accompany you on the day; mine were Baroness Lola Young and Baroness Meral Hussein-Ece. The former Prime Minister was there, and I instinctively hugged, kissed and thanked her.

'I should thank you for what you've done,' May said.

My friends had come down from the balcony and were walking through the vast expanse of Westminster Hall. As they were walking in, Theresa May was going in the opposite direction. Now, my friends don't tend to meet prime ministers, it's just not what they do. And yet that there she was walking towards them. None of my best friends had been to university and there they were in the House of Lords, bumping into the former PM. Gary wasted no time and said, 'Excuse me, Former Prime Minister, we're Simon's best friends and family. I just want to thank you for doing what you've done for my best friend.'

I think she was a little taken aback but she was very gracious. Gary quickly introduced Luca as my son and May said good afternoon to him. Then she wished us all a great day and was gone. It was very special and my friends could hardly believe it.

I made my maiden speech on 31 October, as custom dictates you must deliver before you're allowed to vote in the Lords. It is expected to be less than ten minutes and it's an opportunity to thank the people who have supported you and tell the House something about who you are and what you stand for. Ordinarily, I don't write speeches because it's not the way I feel I best perform. But for a maiden speech, in the House of Lords – for that I almost needed to be word perfect, rather than pitch perfect, which is when you're speaking without notes. I didn't want to risk losing the thread or getting overwhelmed so I thought I'd better write it down.

I guess my big statement of intent was that I believed it was incumbent upon me and upon us as parliamentarians to recognise that talent exists in every street in every city in every corner of the United Kingdom and that it is our job to ensure that potential talent has a pathway to success. I tried to tell a few jokes; I tried to be myself. And of course I thanked my mum, who, I explained to the assembled peers, taught me to have good manners and respect, to fight for myself and to fight for others.

* * *

While it was and remains a huge honour, being ennobled felt strange on many levels, not least because for twenty-five years I'd been an outsider, lobbying, campaigning, protesting and complaining, pointing the finger at the very establishment that now, in one fell swoop, I found myself unexpectedly part of. For nearly sixty years, I'd simply been Simon Woolley; Simon Woolley without a pension, even having to raise my own salary, and that for all the members of OBV, and sometimes not having a salary at all, perennially looking over a financial cliff. For an age that had been my daily diet. And now it was my job to scrutinise legislation: a parliamentarian, a Lord, for heaven's sake, inside the big House.

I still feel that it's slightly ironic that I have railed against the British hierarchical system and yet now here I am, a part of this historical institution, which, little more than sixty years ago, was made up exclusively of men who had inherited their right to be there from fathers, uncles, grandfathers, or who were clergy. But the opportunities I have to move the dial, to bring the politics of fairness, opportunity and dignity into the heart of government, cannot be underestimated. For many Black people, seeing someone like me in this place, talking about the issues that they care about, is a great joy, a great sense of pride. A relief, even.

Sitting on select committees is one way that I can influence government policy for the better, I hope. For example, the Youth Unemployment Committee, on which I sit, is very important because it's mapping out the future for a generation of disadvantaged young people and how they get into work. This is of course a huge privilege, even if a tension between my inner activist and my role as a parliamentarian always remains. In fact, I hope it does, as to me, that is a very good thing that keeps me focused on doing good work. But some of the older readers will know the likes of Lord Ken Clarke, and Lord Ken Baker, big political beasts, both were architects of our modern-day education. For people like me you only saw then on TV: *Question Time*, or coming and going from Downing Street on the news. Now they were my peers, asking my advice about how we shape the next fifty years for young people to excel. Mad, no! Oh, but rest assured, as much I was in awe, I still told them my views, and to their credit, they listened to me and agreed. I'm very proud of that report. I think this is what Theresa May wanted, when she put me here. I know it's what the Black community wanted: 'Simon, you're our voice.' No pressure.

As for the title itself, I am ambivalent about it. On the one hand, it's been utterly transformative in terms of the access you get, the respect and the opportunities. Though there's part of me that rails against people looking up to anyone simply because they have a title. To which my own reflective response is, 'OK, Woolley, raise your game, think, be humble, but deliver.' The humility comes from reminding myself what my ex-colleague and dear friend Merlene Carrington told me when she became a magistrate: 'It's a cloak that I wear – something that's been bestowed on me but is not me, it's part of what I do.' So I use Merlene's wise words with my own twist. It's a cloak that I wear, that bestows upon me superhuman powers to do extraordinary things for our society. But I know that I am Simon Woolley, a social justice and race equality activist. When I go into the chamber, I put that cloak on and I'm Lord Woolley, and then I take it off and I'm Simon again.

When you enter the Lords, there's almost no training. We had one afternoon, and wonderful but limited official support, particularly from Kate and the Head of the Crossbench group Lord Igor Judge, a former High Court judge. I know, you can't make it up.

But across the House I've been shown so much goodwill, it is truly heartening. It's almost as though they'd been waiting for me. Many people approached me, wishing me well and giving me their cards, telling me to get in touch if I needed any help. But the big gap was, you don't get a legislative handbook or anything like that to tell you how it all works. You just have to watch, listen, ask and learn, and hopefully, you start to get the hang of it. Well, that's OK if you're in the House of Lords, as a life peer you've got the rest of your life to learn, the trouble is that it's the same with the House of Commons too. It could take a couple of years or more to learn the ropes and then there's an election and you could be out.

And then there's the point of those who, like me as a Charter 88 volunteer, argued for a democratically elected upper chamber. So now I, as a turkey, might not be in a rush to vote for Christmas, let's get that out of the way! What I hadn't expected in this chamber is the possibility for unbelievable debate about some of the deepest, most challenging issues of the day. As a newbie, I'd go into the chamber and just listen to the debate and speeches, and think, *That's a good point*, then the opposition view, *Never thought about that, great point*. And watching this myriad of views test an argument to destruction. That's a good thing – if an argument can stand up after being tested in this way, then it's a strong one. The other good point is the fact that many of the politicians, particularly those more senior ones that have been in the House of Commons, while still partisan, won't sell their soul. Sell for what, I guess? They are already in the House of Lords. But I'm constantly reminded that the Lords must choose its battles carefully, and respect the will of the Commons vote, before another Dominic Cummings rocks up and threatens to banish the Lords to … where was it? York? That was it.

It is also a source of pride and joy for me that Black staff in the Palace of Westminster look upon me as one of their own. Many know of my backstory campaigning for race equality and have said, 'Lord Woolley, we're so pleased you're here.' I've had polite greetings, fist bumps, handshakes, high fives, hugs, even, from people I've encountered around the Estate who wanted to talk to me. I would say to them, 'I've got your back. You need to have my back too, by the way.' And they'd say, 'One hundred per cent – you got it.'

But for all the goodwill, help and welcome I have received from all quarters when I joined this historic institution, I am aware that, as a person of colour, I am very much in a minority here. Far more than I would be, were I an MP. It is estimated that 6 per cent of members of the upper House come from an ethnic minority background. I am aware of this fact partly because I have been made aware.

The library at the House of Lords is exquisite. It feels like every political book, magazine and journal is there, and you can order anything else you need. It's just a wealth of knowledge, exclusively for the use of peers. Before we were all sent home and everything went online due to the pandemic, I'd often work in there. One day, I got a tap on the shoulder from a fellow peer, who said, 'Excuse me, could you help me with some photocopying, please?' I looked at him and glanced at the library staff to my left. I got up.

'Yes, OK, I'll help you,' I said. Trying to mask my exasperation that he probably thought I was a library staff member, not a peer just like him, I got up out of my seat and helped him with the photocopying. All the while I was thinking, *what am I doing?* But I gave him a pass, more for my own preservation than anything else.

'Thank you,' he said.

I went back to my chair. It was like a Galton and Simpson sketch.

'Did I see correctly what just happened?' asked the Baroness I'd been sitting beside when I'd been approached to lend IT support.

'Yes, you did.'

'He thought you were a member of staff, not a peer.'

'I know, I know.'

'Why didn't you say anything?'

'I was gobsmacked, so I just helped him.'

I didn't say anything because I was new and taken aback. But then it happened again, with another peer.

This time, I said, 'I'm not staff, you know?'

To which the answer came back, 'Oh, yes. No, no, I didn't, er . . . Yes, I did know that . . .'

'OK,' I groaned, 'don't worry, it's fine. It's *fine.*'

And off he went to bother the actual staff.

In both instances, I was wearing my badge. The thing about the Westminster Estate is that the hierarchy is coded into everyone's personal details on their badge. You can tell who they are simply by glancing at the colour on their identification. But these people didn't even bother to check before asking me to help them, they just looked at my face.

It then happened for a third time. This time I just pointed at my badge and said, 'Peer' and then pointed at the library staff and said 'Library support', and he abruptly turned around and walked off sheepishly.

So while there is a lot of goodwill, these events demonstrate to me that some peers just can't see me as one of them. Oh, and I've been called Bill Morris a few times. I love Bill Morris, the nation's first Black General Secretary of a trade union, but he's about twenty years my senior. But there you go – Black men are a rare breed in the House of Lords.

What do you do in a situation like that? As most people of colour will know, when you call out any racism, you know there's a risk that it could turn very badly for you, even as the victim. It's a reason Black people keep schtum.

Most human beings prefer to avoid conflict; we are social animals, evolutionarily conditioned to fit in. Challenging someone, calling them out, takes up so much energy and becomes exhausting. And then there's that part of the Black experience that's wanting to be loved in an unloving world. In a world that – if you accept the argument put forward by the late philosopher Charles W. Mills in his wonderful book, *The Racial Contract* – is in part governed by a racial hierarchy, there are no prizes for guessing who's at the top and who's at the bottom.

But perhaps one of the toughest things to deal with since the knighthood and becoming a Lord isn't actually experiences like those in the library, it has been the 'friendly fire'. A sense from some quarters within the Black and Asian communities of 'Why him, why not me?' That has been not so much hurtful but more disappointing. Because I've spent most of my adult life nurturing and empowering others, actively working to get them into positions of power. And then, at the last hurdle, I myself was put in a privileged position of influence – which seems to have proved challenging to some people.

The other thing to remember is, I suppose it's not unlike the Wild West of Twitter, where you can get a thousand positive responses to something you say and ten negative ones. And yet you find yourself, along with Twitter's algorithms that love conflict, focusing on the negative.

I learned a little bit about how to deal with this from the Reverend Sharpton, who said to me, 'These individuals criticising you may have believed they were better than you or smarter than you in some way. And yet, for whatever reason, it didn't work out for them. So rather than praise you, they want to run you down. And that's more about them than you.' He's right about that. Rather than say, 'I'm pleased one of us has done well,' which most do, this type of person, who has seen themselves as superior, channels their disappointment into criticism. There's a good expression I heard recently – energy vampires. Their survival is based on sucking up positive energy and turning it into something mean. But if you ignore them, then they've got no more fuel and their negativity can't survive, at least around you.

But there's also a lot of love; I see that every day, in one way or another. And that's what I try to remember. I have been very lucky with the friends and allies I have made and they help fuel my determination to carry on with my work, using whatever tools are available to me. My view is that the traditional institutions that govern and shape our country are organic – they're made, and you can unmake, or dramatically reform them. But you can only do that if you're on the inside, reshaping, renewing, saying what needs to be said.

I spend a limited time in the Lords. Head of Homerton is a full-time role, which during term time often begins at 8am and finishes after another formal dinner at 10pm. Oxbridge colleges love a formal dress-up-to-the-nines dinner. Actually, so do I – but please don't tell anyone or we'll have even more!

I finally got the job at Homerton after about twelve interviews, all of them conducted online, and a final election by the Fellows. When the decision came through, I'm told it was a big majority, no need for a second round of votes, some fellows cried, including men, because it was a historic moment – the first Black man to be elected Head of an Oxbridge college. My guess is that Homerton, with its roots in radical preachers from the East End of London over 250 years ago, was just waiting for me. And I in turn was waiting for Homerton. Timing is everything.

One of the Fellows said to me, 'We know you're an activist, but you're also a politician, and a changemaker. You're very welcome here.'

Eight weeks into the job, we had the future king Prince Charles visit, then Civil Rights icon the Reverend Jesse Jackson flew over to receive an honorary fellowship. Another Fellow came up to me and said, 'Simon, you're like a whirlwind.' I smiled politely, and thought, *I'm not even out of second gear yet.*

The gift of Homerton is not just the wonderful estate with its collection of old and new buildings, it's the people within it. In my first few weeks I worked with almost every single department in the college. The cooks, cleaners, maintenance, the gardeners, the Fellows, events team, and above all the students. One cleaner told me, that she'd been there for over thirty years and I was her fourth principal. She said most of them didn't even know her name, 'much less get on their hands and knees and scrub the floor with us'.

I said, 'If I don't scrub the floor with you, how I am going to get all the gossip about what really matters in this place?' She laughed.

Being the first Black male Head here can be daunting, but it's worth it. I had a student come up to me to say, 'Simon, can I call you Simon? You have no idea what your presence means to someone like me. A third-year graduate who walks about this college and others and there are no pictures or paintings with people who look like you and me. And no very senior people. Then you arrive, with your "We're going to change the world" stuff you always talk about.' Her words showed me that representation matters, that my presence as Head of an Oxbridge college matters. It shows other kids from underrepresented backgrounds that changing attitudes is possible. That day, speaking to that student, I wanted to cry, and I think she did too. Feeling very moved as I walked away, I thought, *Someone has put me here to do extraordinary things. So I'd better get on and do them.*

Above all, I tell the students three things as often as I can. One: they belong. Let's have no more imposter syndrome. Two: we will support their drive for academic excellence. And three: we want the education, the values, the friendship that they get from here, to do extraordinary things, for themselves, for others, for society.

I mean, how lucky am I to be helping over 800 students live their most extraordinary lives? It's an incredible – and humbling – honour.

EPILOGUE

So where am I today? I spend a lot of my time in the Lords. I spend term time in Cambridge, at Homerton College, feeling my way into my new role as principal, hoping to shake things up a little. During my first term here, the Reverend Jesse Jackson let me know that he was coming to the UK. It was all pretty new and I was still getting to know the staff. They were surprised when I said he'd be visiting in a couple of weeks and that I hoped to get the approval of my dons to grant him a fellowship. I wanted to extend the kind of welcome to the Reverend that he had to me, all those years ago. And the point is that now I can. I can invite a brother to come to my college, and I can honour the man in the way that he should be. It meant an awful lot to me to have him there, and to be able to bestow this fellowship on him. The Reverend Jesse Jackson was a huge idol for me from when I was a kid. It was Pele, Dr Martin Luther King, and the Reverend Jesse Jackson.

Ever since the first time that I met him in 2012, we found this amazing connection and we've become good friends. Our friendship is now such that every time he has come to the UK in the past ten years, we've met up. And so here I am now, at Homerton, still finding my way as principal. I looked at our list of fellows and it was virtually all white. And so I said to the senior team, this will be my first fellowship and it will be a statement of intent. This is a Black man of immense global standing, whose record on human rights and equality has been essential to improving millions of lives in America. Not only that, he's a role model for so many Black men and women across the world. And the thing is that the Reverend Jesse Jackson was incredibly moved, because this was the first university fellowship he had ever received in the UK. Together, we made history and I'm so proud that this was one of my first acts as principal.

And then not long after that, I was given a fellowship myself, by Magdalen College Oxford, founded 850 years ago, and one of the oldest and most prestigious colleges in the world. Magdalen is so beautiful, with its chapel, the cloisters, it's hard not to feel in awe of the beauty, the serenity, which almost feels spiritual. Its history is extraordinary: Oscar Wilde and T.E. Lawrence (to name just two) studied there. I'm a council estate kid who came to education late, but they now wanted what I have, what I stand for. It meant so much to me. To me, it's about the symbolism of a working-class kid being necessary to the establishment, and that necessity is born out of the activism that I've been a part of my whole adult life. This stuff isn't about me, I accept it, I'm there, because in doing so I'm changing the picture of modern Britain. I'm making a difference. And this is what I said during my speech at Magdalen: I love being a fellow of this college, which has stood for excellence of all kinds for centuries, but my heart is in opportunity, equality for all. And so I've accepted this honour in the spirit of equality – I see this in some ways as a trade off.

Recently, I also had another first, in a period of my life in which I keep on finding myself surprised. I've never visited Barbados, country of birth of my biological mother Lolita and my birth father, who I never knew. Never had the time, never really had a reason to go. Until I got a call from HRH Prince Charles' team asking if I'd be there to mark the moment when Barbados became a republic. What could I say? I've always wondered about this country that is a key part of my heritage, and so I found myself on a flight, arriving at the same time as the Prince's team. Another first, another remarkable few days. I was proud to be there and take part in these historic celebrations. But something very special happened to me right at the end of my visit, which I was not expecting. I accompanied the Prince when he went with the Prime Minister, Mia Mottley, to the National Archives. The Prince went to introduce me to her, and she said, 'I know who you are. Principal of Homerton, Peer. And a bit of an activist too.' She had my number.

Then she told me that she had a surprise for me. On a table in the records room, they'd laid out documents relating to my mother, born Lolita Gibson: her birth certificate, details about the village of her birth. And I stood there looking at the evidence of who my mother was, details I'd never had at my fingertips, which showed me my heritage, and I was with the Prime Minister and the future King of England. I had tears in my eyes. What a journey.

A final scene. I'm asked to be at a dinner for Hillary Clinton, organised by a major international news network; bring your A game, I'm told. No pressure: Hillary Clinton is a hero of mine. She should have been the 45th President of the United States, she should have been the first woman president. She was a brilliant secretary of state under Barack Obama, and her poise in handling a stolen election, and the work she is doing now, are an inspiration to us all. So off I go to the dinner, and to my enormous surprise, I'm seated next to her. And the other guests are heads of news networks, fellow peers, people of note. And for a moment I wonder all over again what the hell I'm doing there. Hillary Clinton asks that we all go around the table and introduce ourselves. As I'm waiting my turn, I think carefully about how to describe myself. And in the end, when it's my turn, I know just what I want to say:

'My name is Simon Woolley, and I'm a political activist.'

Simon Woolley
London and Cambridge
May 2022

ACKNOWLEDGEMENTS

When you've worked locally, nationally, and globally as I have for nearly thirty years in the arena of social and racial justice, you meet a lot of people and you make a lot of friends. Remembering them all now is, of course, mission impossible. Here's a deal. Let me do my best now, and if I forget, you'll remind me, and then when we go to paperback I'll amend the error. Deal? Deal!

First off, the team from Bonnier books. Perminder Mann. For a time she was the only Black or Asian CEO of a top publisher, and that's how we met, in the making of 'The Colour of Power'. Perminder, thank you for inviting me to tell me story. And your team: Margaret Stead, Justine Taylor, Nikki Mander, Jess Tackie, and my super-brother David Matthews. I can't thank all of you enough. Patience, great spirit, guidance, heavy-lifting, light-lifting, and warmth all wrapped up in one.

My OBV family: Rita Patel, Dave Weaver, Audrey Adams, Meena Dhobi, Lee Jasper, Ashok Viswanathan, Merlene Carrington, Rafiq Maricar, Francine Fernandes, Winsome Grace Cornish, Mayowa Adodele, Sandra Stewart, Leon Green, Faz Hakim.

And the volunteers, too long to mention. You all made OBV the institution that it is and you'll continue to make it a beacon for hope and a place to progress.

Now, in no particular order, thanks to: Joe Montgomery, Lester Holloway, Leroy Logan, Herman Ouseley, Arif Ali, Paulette Simpson, Karen Chouhan, Justin Moore, Yvonne Powell, Ann Flintham, James Gomez, Fiona Cannon, Ngaire Woods, Chris Stone, Afua Hirsch, Matthew Ryder, Marcus Ryder, Ray Anderson, Graham Hart, Savvas Demetriou, Mick Wright, Maria Hipwell, Robin Cleveland, Harriet Konisha, Maxine Albert, Jennifer Crook, Zeljko Jovanovic, Kinga Rethy, George and Alex Soros, Hugh Muir, Joseph Harker, Martina Milburn, Michael Hastings, Meral Hussein-Ece, Lola Young, Jenny Jones, John Bercow, Nick Timothy, Kate Macmillan, Parag Mehta, Kurt Barling, Sadiq Khan, Reena Ranger, Marsha de Cordova, Nadine White, Anna Rothery, Beverley Knight, Helen Grant, Alisa Flemming, Serena Simmons, Bernadette Thompson, Marvin Rees, Lora Berg, Sarah Chu, Eva Willams, Oruj Defoite, Alan Edwards, Usha Prasher, Naomi Campbell, Michael Eboda, Ozwald Boateng, David Harewood, Iqbal

Wahhab, Stephen Maynard, Shai Weiss, Tom Ilube, Viv Ahmun, Nero Ughwujabo, David Lammy, Clive Lewis, Francesca Klug, Paul Pearson, Alfiaz Vaiya, Joanna Summer, Keith Vaz, Diane Abbott, Gary Soloff, Shabir Randeree, Sayeeda Warsi, Steven Sylvester, Barbara Lindsay, Tan Dhesi, Helen Grant, Shami Chakrabarti, Momudou Jallow, Sara Sewell, Leila McKenzie-Delis, Magnus Djaba, Larissa Vince, Halima Begum, Mischa Thompson, Lucy Aitkens, Dave Pearson, Steve Howell, Juliette Alexander, Roy Ledgister, Milton Inness, Reverend Al Sharpton, Baroness Floella Benjamin DBE, Caitlin Tickell, Hugh Harris, Balraj Singh, Will Tanner, Jeremy Crook, Karen Blackett, Begona Juarros, David Miliband.

Special thanks must go to the Reverend Jesse Jackson – friend, mentor, hero.